FREE TO WRITE

Free to Write:

Prison Voices Past and Present

Edited by Gareth Creer, Hannah Priest and Tamsin Spargo

Foreword by Erwin James

HEADLAND

First published in 2013
by
HEADLAND PUBLICATIONS
38 York Avenue
West Kirby
Wirral CH48 3JF

ISBN 978 1 902096 14 8

A CIP record for this book is available from the British Library

Designed and typeset by Hannah Priest

Cover design by Rob Shedwick
Cover image copyright © 2013 Rob Shedwick

Printed and bound in Great Britain by
Oriel Studios Digital Ltd.
Orrell Mt.
Bootle
Merseyside L20 6NS

Contents

Editors' Note

Gareth Creer, Hannah Priest and Tamsin Spargo

We are all trapped in our own stories and the beauty of working with writers in prison is that by developing that awareness of our own situation, so the process of writing can help inmates imagine a better outcome for themselves. With a pen and piece of paper, and a little encouragement, anybody can write a different ending.

In introducing new writing by inmates as well as true stories of how writing helped men and women of the past imagine a future beyond prison, Free to Write has produced a book for the prisoner preparing to resume life on the outside. It is the outcome of a practical research project run by Liverpool John Moores University in association with prisons and probation services.

Free To Write
Room 108, Redmonds Building
Liverpool John Moores University
Clarence Street
Liverpool L3 5UG

Foreword

Erwin James

WHOEVER YOU ARE AND however long your sentence, in prison you live inside your head. You're a stranger among strangers, an outcast among outcasts banished to an island of shame built of concrete and steel, where fear is the common currency and pain and struggle abound. A minor altercation with a neighbour can turn into full scale psychological war. An innocent remark or a nod in the wrong direction can lead to violence of the most serious kind. On the blocks, the wings and the landings, you duck and dive and dodge and swerve doing all you can to survive, all the time trying to keep that carefully hidden little kernel of who you think you are intact.

The vagaries of prison life perplex and confound even the most adept survivor. There are rules on paper designed to constrict and control—but on a prison landing, in a prisoner hierarchy, there are no rules. You have to be in it to appreciate it. To try to make sense of it is to attempt to rationalise the irrational. The key is to try and make sense of yourself. How did you get here? Where are you going? Are you who you want to be? Prison might just be the catalyst for the change you seek.

One way to find the answers is to write. Writing allows you to live a little outside your head, to get an objective perspective on your situation. Thoughts become words on paper. Memories and dreams become poems and narratives that you can form and fashion and upon which you can reflect. Writing in prison can raise a crushed spirit and reignite the embers of hope and might just help you to get to where you want to be—and perhaps more importantly to get to be who you really want to be.

The Free to Write Project has demonstrated that the long, rich and resilient tradition of writing in prison is as vital and vibrant as ever. The poems and narratives within these pages tell us of lives that are valuable and relevant. The writers may have fallen from grace, but their words are a timely and poignant reminder of that most obvious of truths—they are the words, not of prisoners, but of people in prison.

Reading them brought me pleasure and reminded me how much I owed the richness of my post-prison life to writing. When I walked out of the prison gates after serving my twenty years it felt like I was crawling out of a hole as deep as a mountain. Without a pencil and paper I might never have made it. To everyone who champions, promotes and supports writing in prison I wish courage, strength and good fortune. I wish the same to those in prison who choose to write. A prisoner may be a captive: confined, regulated and controlled. But a prisoner who can think and breathe will always be free to write.

Free to Learn? Reading and Writing in the Early Nineteenth-Century Prison

Helen Rogers

The Bank of England's £5 note depicts an iconic moment in the history of the prison—Elizabeth Fry reading the Bible to women prisoners and their children, warders and Christian visitors at Newgate Gaol in 1816, all of whom are listening intently to the Quaker philanthropist. It reminds us that reading—and to a lesser extent writing—was at the heart of early attempts to reform the prison and its

Reproduced with permission of the Bank of England

inmates. Christian teaching would 'soften' and 'civilise' prisoners, reformers claimed, making them susceptible to repentance and rehabilitation. In this context, reading and writing were not about individual freedom of expression, enquiry and creativity, but the perceived need of prisoners for religious instruction and salvation in order to begin new and better lives.[1] What, then, might these early experiments in prison learning have to tell us about current projects like Free to Write and the kinds of liberation they might inspire?[2]

Many creative projects in prisons today are run by volunteers from outside the penal sector, but their success depends on active cooperation between prisoners and staff, and sharing and respect between all participants. The achievements of Fry and other 'lady visitors' in improving the treatment of female inmates at Newgate Gaol likewise depended on collaboration with women prisoners who actively requested education. They complained repeatedly of the 'Want of Employment', for example, and that being 'compelled to be idle, and that having nothing else to do, they were obliged to pass away the time doing wrong'. Though Fry had intended only to establish a school for their children, the women persuaded her to provide them with needlework and teach them to read and write.[3]

Fry earned the Newgate prisoners' trust by involving them in decision-making and the learning process. They elected one woman prisoner to be Schoolmistress, and others as classroom monitors. Nevertheless, they had to agree to the teaching plan and rules drawn up by the ladies. While today the content of reading and writing workshops in prisons is usually negotiated by participants, at Newgate, as in all nineteenth-century gaols, prisoners only had access to literature approved by their teachers. Principally this was the Bible, supplemented by religious and moralistic fables. Yet, when asked to vote to accept Fry's rules, by a show of hands the prisoners unanimously renounced their own sources of amusement—playing cards, singing, dancing, 'dressing up in men's clothes' and reading novels—in return for Bible reading, learning to write and needlework.[4] What motivated these women to give up their games, bawdy songs and racy stories for sober instruction?

From the copious writings of Fry and her followers we learn a lot about what Christian instruction meant to prison philanthropists. Only occasionally, however, did they mention what prisoners actually said and we have to read between the lines to get a glimpse of what prison education may have meant to these students. Useful employment, learning to read and write, and concern for their children, were certainly powerful incentives for the Newgate women. The varied responses of inmates to religious instruction, ranging from willing to oppositional, are more evident, however, in the prison journals of Sarah Martin, who started visiting Great Yarmouth Gaol in 1818. Unlike most prison visitors, Martin was a dressmaker who lived in the crowded narrow rows around the gaol that housed Yarmouth's labouring poor, including many of her prison scholars. As a working woman, living in close contact with offenders and their families, she was acutely aware of the hardships they faced though, for her, these never excused their crimes. Until Martin died in 1843, she kept a daily record of the lessons she ran and monitored her students' progress before and after release. Despite their pious and often judgemental tone, her prison journals provide rare insights into the short- and longer-term benefits that reading and writing, no matter how didactic, could have for the convicted.[5]

Some inmates appear to have been moved by Christian instruction and found comfort and lasting support in the Bible. The teacher gave many a Testament or hymnbook on their departure and Eleanor Simmonds, who stayed in touch with Martin, kept her copy to give her eldest child. Some urged their fellow prisoners to heed the teacher. At the end of their sentences, for instance, a group of smugglers addressed the prisoners in chapel 'and entreated them to listen to [Martin's] advice, and treat her with respect'. Subsequently, as they reported to their former teacher, all left the smuggling trade.[6]

Most inmates had only basic skills in literacy, if any. For working-class children at this time schooling was very basic, brief and often interrupted by the need to work. Many prisoners therefore seized a rare opportunity to learn. In thirty days, one young man 'improved greatly in reading [...] and made good advance in writing'. As a child he had tried making his letters with chalk but had 'never before attempted to use a pen' and 'gladly accepted instruction'. Some took pride in their learning and thanked their teacher. William Smith, having learned to read and write during his six-month sentence, spent his last week preparing a copybook for his tutor. Even those who were unconfident and easily distracted could take pride in learning. The boy William Tunmore was frequently in trouble with the gaoler and struggled to remember the alphabet. But when he was ill and alone in the infirmary, Martin wrote out verses for the warder to read to him and, on discharge, Tunmore asked to keep them to show his father.[7]

Instruction and occupation must have been particularly welcome to foreign prisoners who found themselves in an alien and bewildering environment. A Flemish prisoner used his time to write an account of his life. A Frenchman could read and write in his own language but spoke no English: 'He eagerly learned to read the New Testament in English—was greatly interested in that book. It occupied the whole of his attention.' Understanding the comfort the Bible brought to some inmates, a former prisoner sympathised with the plight of a German prisoner, for he gave Martin a German Bible for his use in exchange for an English copy. The young German's face 'brighten[ed] with pleasure' on receiving the Testament: 'It is a wonderful Book to me.' The following day he had read thirty-three chapters. Martin and the student read the two Bibles alongside each other. Though the prisoner struggled to express himself in English, 'the manner in which he did it was satisfactory'. The teacher noted: 'His memory and natural understanding are good.' In six months he could read in English.

For considerable numbers, Martin's lessons were a distraction from the tedium of 'doing time'. Prison will have been an intimidating environment for many inmates. The gaol's disciplinary records reveal frequent quarrels and fights among prisoners. Raucous inmates were sometimes punished following complaints by other prisoners when their sleep was disturbed by shouting and singing. Some prisoners welcomed the orderly and quiet atmosphere of Martin's lessons and, so they could concentrate on their study, asked the teacher to keep the disruptive juveniles quiet and busy by giving them patchwork. Even the most disengaged scholars could find unexpected pleasure in working with the teacher. During their one-month stay in 1840 a boisterous group of barely literate boys managed, by and large, to settle to their lessons when promised stories if they learned their letters. Picture books were a rare luxury for them—'Oh! what beautiful books!' they gasped. Despite the moralising content, they delighted in stories about 'wicked and naughty' boys like themselves. Each morning they welcomed their teacher at the prison gate to check she had brought them more books. All reoffended but, from Martin's reports of their lessons, there is little doubt of the affection that grew between the teacher and pupils. One boy, who had recently lost his mother, wept on his departure. '[H]e says he likes to have you teach him every day', reported another prisoner. 'Would that I had the time to instruct him every day', wrote Martin wistfully, 'and to take care of him'.

From 'The Jail Missionary', in Women of Worth: A Book for Girls, *illustrated by W. Dicks (London: James Hogg, 1859), 51-69 (68)*

Like Elizabeth Fry, Sarah Martin set prisoners to useful work if they showed willing to learn scripture. She helped them find work on release by providing them with tools and materials. This was another powerful incentive to follow her instruction, for many acquired new skills in gaol—carving cutlery out of bone, plaiting straw hats, needlework and mending—and earned money they received on departure. Though Martin saw education and employment as alternatives to what, in her eyes, were the delinquent habits of offenders—gaming, blaspheming, idleness, and so on—in practice prisoners seem to have integrated work and learning into their own inmate culture. The servants Martha and Sarah Carter, charged with thieving from their employers, were typical in their opportunistic use of prison learning and employment. Shortly after admission, Martin found them 'very unable to answer questions from what is read, but very docile and attentive', and she began to teach them writing. Outside lessons, however, they could be loud and insolent and were confined several times for noise and quarrelling. Threatened with the withdrawal of sewing—Martha Carter was making a serge coat and hoping to become a dressmaker—they settled down to study. Within a month, she could memorise up to four verses from *Divine Songs* by Watts (the author of 'Amazing Grace') and was asked to help another prisoner with her lessons. 'It is gratifying to observe how greatly Martha and Sarah Carter improve in reading, and how hard they labour to learn lessons', commented Martin.

On her return from a rare week's absence, the teacher was delighted to find all her scholars had exceeded her expectations. Martha Carter had memorised thirty-eight verses. But though prisoners often encouraged each other in such feats of learning, they also led each other astray. Carter and a cellmate were discovered to have used their sewing materials to make purses for their sweethearts and to have thrown love letters into the male ward, written with materials supplied by Martin. Consequently, the materials were confiscated. Deprived the opportunity to write, Carter lost interest in her lessons:

> Martha Carter is deceitful and idle. I believe that on the moment of hearing the keys at the door she takes her book which has been neglected before. Then

> looking at it and whispering her verses over when placing the book before me she tries to stand so as to see part of it [...] Her books shall be withheld until she attends to what is required of her in this way.

Despite the reprimand, Carter continued to teach her friend a verse each day, an activity she must have enjoyed. Assisting others in their learning was an element of inmate culture and companionability that co-existed with, and yet was independent of, Martin's approved activities. While Martin, like most contemporary penal reformers, feared that prisoners 'contaminated' each other with their 'bad habits', at the same time she recognised they could exert a beneficial influence over each other. Consequently, she strove to channel their enthusiasm for learning by encouraging them to assist each other, as did Martha Carter by teaching her friend.

Sociability, therefore, was one of the major attractions of prison schooling at Yarmouth, and this historical evidence helps to confirm a neglected aspect of arts and creative practice in prisons today. Studies have tended to overlook the role of arts-based approaches to rehabilitation in fostering group ties and identities, emphasising instead their value in nurturing self-expression and individual empowerment. Yet, as Jenny Hartley and Sarah Turvey argue, having facilitated prison reading groups for nearly twenty years, sociability is one of the most important outcomes—and pleasures—of reading together. Reading groups 'allow readers to share experiences of a book, to test out their personal responses against those of other people. They are dynamic encounters and people negotiate and re-think meaning in the process of talking and listening to one another.'[8]

While Sarah Martin's lessons offered little scope for creativity or free discussion, some inmates purloined materials and used newly honed literacy skills to imaginative and subversive ends. Sentenced to transportation, James Brown wrote a six-page letter to his friends outside the gaol to warn them to learn from his example and give up drink and swearing. Though Brown adopted the sorrowful tone found in other criminal and temperance confessions, it is clear from the Gaoler's records that Brown was not bowed by this penitent literature. He used paper that Martin gave him for copying religious sentences to send notes to female inmates. His writing suggests that he enjoyed the psalms which he sang in the prison chapel and memorised in his cell. Lyrical and musical, these may have encouraged his poetic taste for one of his letters consisted of 'three half sheets closely written in verse'. The Gaoler, however, found the content 'obscene'.[9]

Doubtless Brown's verse was influenced too by the ribald songs he used to sing in the alehouse. Singing was a favourite pastime among inmates, leading to punishment when it became too rowdy.[10] Brown's verses proved contentious, provoking a quarrel between two women, resulting in Mary Ann Blyth being struck by a stool. Punished by the removal of paper, Blyth refused food and took to writing on her cell wall, naming the magistrates as her 'murderers' and proclaiming, 'Death pay me a visit'. This was one of several acts of graffiti recorded in the Gaoler's journal, probably aided by pens and chalk provided by Sarah Martin. Later Mary Ann Blyth deployed her literary skills successfully to petition the mayor to be separated from other women and to share a cell with one companion. Blyth's petition and graffiti and Brown's letters and verses confirm that reading and writing were important means of social interaction for those behind the prison walls and tools for individual and group agency.

Though inmates used their prison learning to their own ends, they were reluctant to see it jeopardised. Many complained about the religious content of their schooling and resented being required to memorise scripture before they were allowed storybooks or taught to write. The young father, Francis James, declared he had no desire to read the Bible and wanted only to learn to write: 'I wont [*sic*] believe a word of it. It is all nonsense; victuals is what I want.' His cellmates murmured assent. 'We don't want religion. We want victuals.' As on other occasions when her authority was challenged, Martin threatened to withdraw her services if the scholars refused instruction. Support for the rebel evaporated and the students begged Martin to return. The following day all knew their lessons and sought their teacher's approval by discussing God's existence. It is likely they encouraged Francis James to re-join the class, for soon he told Martin he wished to learn, bring up his children as 'good Christians', and please his wife by avoiding the alehouse. Martin thought his new religious outlook genuine for he took to 'reclaiming' fellow prisoners and was never again convicted.[11]

The stand-off between Francis James and Sarah Martin illustrates not only the importance of peer-pressure in the success of prison schooling but also the vital role played by families in motivating prisoners to acquire learning. A smuggler 'entirely learned to read and write in gaol'. On discharge he abandoned smuggling and sailed between London and Dunkirk selling butter and eggs. In his many letters to Martin 'he expressed the comfort he found in being able to write' to his wife. Some women were keen to thank Martin for teaching their husbands or sons. In a typical example, Arthur Bland's wife reported more than two years after his release that 'it was a good thing her husband learned to read in the jail, as he now takes up a book of an evening; and it was a good thing he learned to write too, because he can now keep his accounts, and write his milk bills'. Literacy enabled Bland to support his family more effectively. But Mrs Bland implied that reading had helped steady her husband's character and kept him away from the pub where, like many men in this hard-drinking port, he had previously drunk his wages. Since discharge, according to Martin, Bland had 'conducted himself well towards his family, and borne an honest conduct'.[12]

Evidence from Martin's papers suggests considerable numbers of former prisoners kept in contact with the teacher and assured her their prison education had made a difference to them. Some who had been resistant to instruction later thanked her for her kindness. Thomas Anderson, sentenced to transportation, had been 'fond of taverns and gaming' before his conviction. During six months at Yarmouth Gaol he ignored Martin's guidance and she frequently found him playing cards. Only in the month before he was sent to the hulks did he pay her attention and 'heartily expressed his thanks'. But from Van Diemen's Land, when he had nothing to gain from the teacher, he wrote to Martin, wishing her success in instructing prisoners.[13]

Martin's account of the convict Thomas Anderson echoes an incident related in the first published account of the work of Elizabeth

Fry and the lady visitors at Newgate Gaol. Fearing the prisoners continued playing cards, Fry asked the women to hand over their packs, out of kindness to their teachers, if not for their own sakes. Five women dutifully relinquished their cards and were rewarded for their honesty with a new muslin handkerchief. One girl, however, 'looked disappointed'. She had hoped, she said, for a Bible with her own name written inside it, 'which she should value beyond anything else, and always keep and read'.[14] Fry interpreted the girl's wish as evidence of the purifying nature of Christian kindness. In the light of the varied responses of inmates to religious instruction at Yarmouth, we might be more cautious in our interpretation of this incident. Did the girl feel under pressure to prove her commitment to reform? Maybe she was trying to gain approval, more employment, a good report? Perhaps the student was cleverly outwitting her teacher by claiming the moral high ground? Or did she simply long for a book of her own, with her name in it, which perhaps only now she could read or write?

The episode probably inspired Jerry Barrett's painting *Mrs Fry Reading to the Prisoners in Newgate, in the year 1816* (1863) upon which the Bank of England's £5 note is based. In the centre of the picture, Elizabeth Fry looks intently at two women, while pointing to the Bible, as if she is appealing directly to them. The women stand arm-in-arm. One, we are to be in no doubt, is a fallen woman who will have plied her body on the same streets from which she must have stolen, for her dress falls Magdalene-like off her shoulder and she looks shamefully at the floor. The other woman appears to be consoling her, yet behind her friend's back she is concealing from Mrs Fry's penetrating gaze a pack of cards. At their feet, two young boys, perhaps their children, are playing dice, an ominous sign of future gambling. Behind them, while some women are listening and weeping, others are gossiping over a bottle of porter.[15]

Barrett's painting intended to portray what many saw as the 'astonishing' success of the Quaker ladies in 'taming the wild beasts' of Newgate.[16] For sceptics, however, the unruly scene to the right of the picture will have confirmed their view that thieves and miscreants, who lived by their wits, were unlikely to be redeemed by religious teaching

Reproduced with permission of the Trustees of the British Museum

and kindly exhortation. Surely, they asserted, wily offenders knew only too well how to dissemble to their gullible teachers, as did Charles Dickens in his satirical portrayal of the 'ever so humble' 'reformed' prisoner, Uriah Heep, in *David Copperfield* (1850). While Christian instruction was a central plank of penal reform and prison discipline in the early decades of the century, by the 1850s critics began to challenge the figures produced by gaol chaplains that claimed to prove the link between religious instruction and desistance from crime. Pessimism began to win out and there was little place in the mid-Victorian regime of 'hard bed, hard fare, hard work' for the humanitarian approach to reading portrayed by Barrett in his Newgate painting.[17]

It is telling, therefore, that the Bank of England £5 note celebrating the work of prison reformers like Fry conceals the disreputable side of Barrett's prison room with the watermark. Instead of the two 'fallen' girls, a seated woman bends maternally over the two small boys at her feet. This sanitised version of the original nineteenth-century painting suggests the controversy and nervousness that is still engendered by rehabilitative approaches to correction. There is considerable recognition in prisons and policy-making groups that creative arts projects can play a vital role in helping prisoners acquire new skills and more expansive aspirations, and relinquish anti-social and self-destructive behaviour. In competing for limited resources and funding, however, projects like Free to Write are expected to provide evidence of successful rehabilitation. Such outcomes, as Sarah Martin knew from twenty-five years of voluntary prison work, are difficult to measure and evaluate.

Tracking the conduct of her former scholars, as they appeared to tread the straight-and-narrow or slip away from it, Sarah Martin girded herself against despair, especially when some returned to gaol. She found hope in the parable of the sower who was 'rewarded, when, by a power not his own, the grain arises, and is still nourished by the sun and the rain from heaven'.[18] A prayer, a hymn, a Bible story might be heard and forgotten but who could say when and how it might be remembered? Thomas Anderson found something, eventually, in his prison schooling that helped him forge a new life in Australia with his wife and children he had sent for from England. Similarly, the value of Free to Write and similar projects for participants may lie in the future as much as in the present. It can never be fully quantified, for such experiences are beyond calculation. While historical evidence from Yarmouth and Newgate gaols reveals the importance of hope and optimism in approaches to rehabilitation, it also suggests that these are most effective when teachers and facilitators work in partnership with learners. Though Martin and Fry sought to replace the games and stories of inmates with their purer, Godly culture, these need not have been alternatives. Yarmouth's prisoners continued to sing their own songs even when they relished Martin's hymns. Creative art in prison should enable participants to value their own culture as much as it opens up new sources of enrichment and understanding.

Notes

1 For more discussion of this image and Fry's work at Newgate, see Helen Rogers, 'The Bank of England's £5 note, Elizabeth Fry and the Women of Newgate', 29 April, 2013, on http://crimeinthecommunity.wordpress.com/2013/04/29/the-bank-of-englands-5-note-elizabeth-fry-and-the-women-of-newgate/.

2 For an overview of recent studies of prison reading and writing projects, see Ann Schwan (ed.) *Critical Survey*, 23:3 (2011), Special Issue 'Reading and Writing in Prison'.

3 Thomas Foxwell Buxton, *An Inquiry, Whether Crime and Misery are Produced or Prevented, by Our Present System of Prison Discipline* (London: John and Arthur Arch, 1818), 114, 117, 118-9.

4 *Ibid.*, 123-6.

5 All references are to Sarah Martin's surviving prison journals, covering the years 1836-41, which are held by Great Yarmouth Museum Services. Extracts from the journals can be found in Martin's short memoir, first published after her death in 1844: *Sarah Martin, the Prison Visitor of Great Yarmouth, with extracts from her Writings and Prison Journals, a New Edition with Additions* (London: Religious Tract Society, n.d. [1847]). This chapter also includes information about prisoners and their imprisonment drawn from the records of Great Yarmouth Gaol, held by the Norfolk Record Office.

6 Extracts from Sarah Martin's 'Liberated Prisoners Book', in 1840 [258] *Inspectors of Prisons of Great Britain II, Northern and Eastern District, Fifth Report, House of Commons Parliamentary Papers Online* (2005), 124-31. For more on apparently reformed prisoners, see Helen Rogers, 'Kindness and Reciprocity: Liberated Prisoners and Christian Charity in Early Nineteenth-Century England', *Journal of Social History* (forthcoming, 2014).

7 For more detailed discussion of Martin's prison school, see Helen Rogers, 'The Way to Jerusalem: Reading, Writing and Reform in an Early Victorian Gaol', *Past and Present*, 205 (2009): 71-104; '"Oh What Beautiful Books": Captivated Reading in an Early Victorian Gaol' *Victorian Studies*, 55:1 (2012): 57-84.

8 Jenny Hartley and Sarah Turvey, 'Reading Together: the Role of the Reading Group inside Prison', *Prison Services Journal* (May, 2009).

9 For more on this prisoner, see Rogers, 'Way to Jerusalem'.

10 See Helen Rogers, 'Singing in Gaol: Christian Instruction and Inmate Culture in the Nineteenth Century', *Prison Service Journal*, 199 (January, 2012): 35-43.

11 *Sarah Martin*, 114-8.

12 Extract from Sarah Martin's 'Liberated Prisoners Book', in 1840 [258] *Inspectors of Prisons*.

13 *Ibid.*

14 Buxton, *Inquiry*, 130; *Memoir of the Life of Elizabeth Fry, with extracts from her journals and letters*, ed. by two of her daughters, 2 vols (London: John Hatchard, 1847), vol. 1, 297-8.

15 For more discussion of this painting, see Alison Booth, *How to Make It as a Woman: Collective Biographical History from Victoria to the Present* (Chicago and London: University of Chicago Press, 2004), 147-51.

16 Buxton, *Inquiry*, 133; *Memoir of the Life of Elizabeth Fry*, 261.

17 Norval Morris and David J. Rothman (eds), *The Oxford History of the Prison: the Practice of Punishment in Western Society* (Oxford: Oxford University Press, 1995), chapters by Randall McGowen (71-99) and Seán McConville (117-50).

18 *Sarah Martin*, 24-5.

Mountain Bughouse 216: One Prisoner's Writing as Protest and Escape

Tamsin Spargo

In 1908 a poem was submitted to the *Star of Hope*, a newspaper published for and by prisoners in the New York State prison system. It was a scathing commentary on conditions in the Dannemora State Hospital, an institution for men who had been certified insane as prisoners, and was signed 'Mountain Bughouse 216'. The author was a man who had attempted for nearly twenty years, as a fugitive and as a prisoner, to use the written word for different purposes and with varying degrees of success. This essay explores some facets of his changing relationship with writing and of the vital role writing played for prisoners in his lifetime, as it coincided with attempts to reform the United States' prison system in the early twentieth century.[1] This period saw the first concerted efforts, within the penal system and by reformers, to explore creativity as a means not only of maintaining order in prisons but of aiding rehabilitation. His own circumstances prevented him from benefitting fully from writing in preparing for a better future, but his story demonstrates the possibilities that writing offers to even the most isolated and fragile prisoner.

'Mountain Bughouse 216''s poem was not accepted for publication and it is not hard to see why. In 1908 campaigns in the United States, and in New York State, for prison reform—on the basis of the possibility of rehabilitation for at least some prisoners rather than containment and punishment for all—were gradually gaining ground, and publications like the *Star of Hope* needed to present prisoners in a positive light. The *Star of Hope* had been founded in Sing Sing prison in 1899 in a rare act of co-operation between two often opposed groups in the penal world: the Warden and a Christian campaigner. Usually, Wardens were conservative figures, keen on maintaining traditional practices designed to contain and control convicts, and deeply suspicious of the campaigners who were arguing that the closed worlds of the prison degraded and debased prisoners and keepers alike. At Sing Sing, which was at the time a prison where some reformist principles were adopted, things were different. The title of the paper was a tribute to Maud Ballington Booth, an English-born evangelical campaigner who had started a religious League of Hope among prisoners in Sing Sing in 1896 and whose belief in rehabilitation was summarised in her 1903 book *After Prison—What?*[2] The Warden, who, as the *New York Times* noted, was 'managing editor and censor' of the paper, was Col. Omar Van Leuven Sage, whose work has been connected with the Progressive reform movement within the penal system which attempted to use rational, scientific principles to engage prisoners in productive, improving activities.[3] In the *Star of Hope*, which was distributed throughout the state's many prisons, prisoners could express and exchange views making it a radical departure from the normal regime which isolated and silenced inmates. But as debates within the paper itself showed, its writers needed to be careful about the impression they gave, whether for readers of an evangelical, conservative, or Progressive, liberal bent.[4] If prisoners were to be promoted as rational and thoughtful, capable of either redemption or reform, there were evidently limits to the type of writing, to the subjects and tone that could be included. 'Mountain Bughouse 216''s submission exceeded those limits.

Earlier that same year, on the 18 July, the *Star of Hope* had published a poem by the same prisoner, this time bearing the less contentious name 'Dannemora State Hospital 216'. The poem 'Independence Day' was a stirring call to support the nation's fighting men, written in the form of an acrostic, with the first letters of each line spelling out 'JULY FOURTH NINETEEN HUNDRED AND EIGHT'. It was a poem that aligned the prisoner with values of courage and patriotism that made it an ideal example of the impression reformers wanted to give, but the paper did accommodate some critical views. As the poem's opening lines declare, this was, also, a call for 'Justice': 'Justice sails on every breeze/Under our soldiers' flag.'[5] In common with other contributions to the paper, it invited readers outside the system to see those within it as sharing a belief in common virtues and values, whatever mistakes had been made in the past, and as deserving to have those principles demonstrated within the prison system as well as in wider society. Such prisoners implicitly displayed the possibilities for reform, both of prisoners and of prisons, and the *Star of Hope* is rightly acknowledged as a significant early example of prisoners' writing having a positive impact outside and inside the prison system.[6]

But inmate 216 in the Dannemora State Hospital, Oliver Curtis Perry, had not reformed and was probably incapable of doing so, at least in the terms of his keepers and physicians. Perry had been declared insane as a prisoner and was confined in a facility within the grounds of the most remote prison in New York State. Clinton, aptly known at the time, both for its distance from families and friends and for its terrible winters, as 'Little Siberia', was a notoriously tough prison and the State Hospital once located not far from New York City at Matteawan was relocated there in 1902 in a move that redoubled the isolation of its inmates. It was known, by inmates and popularly, as the 'Mountain Bughouse', and men who were held there as 'bugs'.

Reproduced from the collection of the Library of Congress

Between the submission of the first poem and the second, Perry had been dealt a crushing blow. He had repeatedly appealed against his certification as insane and requested a return to prison to complete his sentence. In this period the Superintendent of Prisons suggested to the Superintendent Physician at Dannemora that Perry be returned to prison for a trial period. The latter refused and Perry was condemned to stay in the 'Mountain Bughouse' indefinitely. Perry's use of the name seems both a bitterly ironic comment and a cry of protest.

Oliver Perry was a determined man and a difficult prisoner. Throughout his twenty-eight years in Dannemora, he mounted sustained protests at the conditions in which he and his fellow inmates were kept, focusing particularly on what he saw as a contradiction inherent in the State Hospital system. If, he argued, he had been declared mentally ill, he should be treated as a patient and granted better food and conditions and he should not be forced to wear the hated prison uniform. In fact, although a small number of trusted prisoners, 'trusties', were allowed some privileges, most were denied basic things like exercise in the open air. He made formal appeals to the Warden, to State Commissions, and wrote to newspapers, repeatedly asking both for a review of his sanity and of the conditions of the men in his institution. When his appeals and requests were turned down, Perry embarked on several overlapping campaigns of direct action.

When his demands for food that was suitable for a man whose digestion and teeth had been ruined by years of prison life were refused, he embarked on a hunger strike. From 1903 until his death in 1930, Perry refused any food that did not suit him and the State Hospital response, standard for the time, was to tie him to a table and feed him through a nasal tube. In addition to this intermittent hunger strike and force feeding, Perry reacted to the authorities' refusal to let him wear clothing other than standard prison uniform by choosing to wear only his underwear and, in his last years, to go naked, even in the sub-zero temperatures of the upstate New York winters. He also, very occasionally, made what would now be called dirty protests when he soiled the floor of his cell because, he claimed, his pot had been hidden or had not been emptied. There was a reason why he was vulnerable to malicious practical jokes and needed better conditions: since 1895 Oliver Perry had been blind.

Perry had destroyed his own eyes, with nails, after repeated and sustained incarceration in the solitary confinement cells in Auburn penitentiary, his first adult prison. In these unheated basement cells, known as 'jails' or 'dungeons', he would have been in total darkness, sleeping on a damp stone floor, crawling with lice and other vermin. His daily rations were a small piece of bread to eat and a small cup of water and, apart from a keeper checking he was alive once a day, he would have had no human contact, hearing only the noises of the prison for weeks on end. The effects of such confinement on a prisoner, no matter how robust his mental health, are easy to imagine; less easy to comprehend is the fact that the prison, where this treatment was meted out for relatively trivial offences such as trying to obtain writing paper or insubordination to a keeper, had once been seen as a model of good practice. Its failure was to be the spur for the Progressive reform movement that would eventually see activities like writing as more effective than forced labour and isolation.

When Auburn was built in 1816 it developed the eponymous 'Auburn' system which was intended to discipline and reform prisoners through a regime of congregate, silent labour in prison workshops and isolation in single cells. The aim was to make prisoners productive but to prevent them from corrupting each other through conversation. Silence and solitude, including being deprived of the right to exercise in outdoor yards or speak in corridors, and the insistence that on Sunday, a day without labour, men were locked in cells for silent contemplation, were intended to encourage solitary reflection on their crimes. It was, in theory, a regime designed to isolate and shape individual prisoners, as well as to make them labour for their keep.[7] In practice, it was unpopular with local industries, because free inmate labour allowed the prisons to undercut them in the market and could only be effective in 'reforming' the small number of prisoners who were not broken by the regime. The lack of any constructive or creative activity or outlet, combined with the effective isolation of prisoners, both institutionalised and hardened the majority. The system was gradually modified through the nineteenth century, including the introduction of some educational schemes, but it was still failing in the twentieth century.[8]

In 1912, eighteen years after Perry suffered the trauma of punishment in the solitary cell, the chairman of the New York State Commission on Prison Reform, Thomas Mott Osborne, later a reforming Warden at Auburn and at Sing Sing, spent a week undercover in Auburn, as inmate 'Thomas Brown'. The book based on his prison experience and diary, *Within Prison Walls*, graphically revealed the physical and psychological brutalities of the 'model' regime and made a powerful case for reform that would focus on preparing prisoners to leave and not return. At the heart of Osborne's response, and his later pioneering work as a prison governor, was the simple question: 'Shall our prisons be scrap heaps or human repair shops?'[9] Osborne's interest in prison reform combined the discourse of Christian and moral conviction of the capability of the prisoner to change in the right conditions with a pioneering determination to understand prisoners' experience and to listen to their (silenced) voices. In whispered conversations and through messages exchanged on scraps of paper, which was how prisoners overcame the rule of silence, Osborne gathered the information he needed to supplement his own experience undercover.

Osborne gathered enough material to call for the radical reform of the system but he had not experienced the most dreaded punishment within the prison, so he deliberately infringed a rule in Auburn to be sent to the dungeon cells. His account of the experience of just one night, and the collapse of reason in such conditions, makes it clear why, after spending forty-four days, over six weeks, in a cell Perry suffered a psychotic episode. But Oliver Perry was extraordinarily resilient, as well as volatile, as his approach to writing as well as crime reveals.

When Perry was sent to Auburn in 1892, he was something of a celebrity criminal, having twice robbed the New York Central's American Express Special train single-handed and evaded capture before being caught after a spectacular chase in steam trains, sleighs and on horseback, which hit the headlines across the world.[10] He was sentenced to fifty years' hard labour, a harsh sentence even by the standards of the day, as nobody was killed in either of his crimes, but Perry's notoriety attracted an exemplary punishment. While Perry was on the run, the press had turned him into a romantic character, part Robin Hood, part dashing villain, and when he was captured he started a dialogue with reporters that he would attempt to continue throughout his life with varying results. Before his trial, and later, whenever he had access to the press, directly or through friends, he gave interviews that ranged from searing critiques of conditions in prison, and of the system, to accounts of his life and the reasons for his crimes. The narrative was one that revealed as much about the injustices and failings of his society, and the prison system, as about his own motivations and Perry's skills as a storyteller, both of fact and of fantasy, were notable.

The man who ended his life as 'Mountain Bughouse 216' had been repeatedly incarcerated in penal institutions since childhood. Homeless after his father's remarriage, he was arrested as a boy for stealing a suit to sell so that he could pay for lodgings. The ironically named Western House of Refuge in Rochester, where he was sent, was exposed soon after for the systematic physical and sexual abuse of boys by keepers, and Perry's own record and subsequent behaviour strongly supports a reading that he was subject to grooming and abuse. An eventual attempt to 'go straight' and a job as a railroad brakeman left him with a head injury sustained while running along the top of a train and a plan to make money by robbing the train. His first robbery was extraordinarily daring and successful but the compulsion that drove Perry to repeat it some months later ended his life as a free man. In his accounts, Perry told a romantic tale of forbidden love that attracted the sympathies of his growing 'fans': he embroidered on time spent in the west to claim that he had fallen for a rancher's daughter and had robbed his first train to pay for a home for them both. In a tragic twist he had, he claimed, travelled west with his new fortune only to find that she had died, and his second crime was out of desperation. Initially presented as credible in the press and by prison reform groups, Perry's stories were eventually dismissed as manipulative, from the perspective of the prison authorities, or as deluded, by his doctors, but he used his skill in creating narratives that appealed to his different readers throughout his life.

To general astonishment Perry escaped from the first State Hospital to which he was committed and managed, after gaining support from Christian and Progressive reformers, to secure a temporary reversal of his certification as insane. His main supporter, Amelia Haswell, was a Christian 'missionary' whose involvement in his case culminated in her being arraigned before a Grand Jury, charged with aiding his escape. Her trial was seen by reformers as an attack on their principles, and she was eventually acquitted, but it also had a dramatic impact on Perry. Returned to Auburn, Perry was, he noted later, wracked with guilt at the arrest of the woman he called 'mother' and his battle with his keepers intensified until a longer spell in the dungeon eventually triggered the psychotic episode and self-blinding that condemned him to what one reporter called his 'Living Tomb'.[11] Whether Perry was suffering from an acute psychiatric disorder, or from psychotic episodes caused by the extreme conditions of the punishment cells, is impossible to determine. Perry evidently believed that his mental condition was the result of his institutional conditions and treatment and he devoted most of his energies, once committed, to campaigning to change them.

Although pro-reform officials showed interest in his cause, Perry's attempts to have his case and conditions reviewed by using the press brought diminishing returns. While conditions for those in the regular prison system were improved as the concept of rehabilitation began to be taken seriously, what Perry called his 'brand of insanity' undermined his arguments. The history of his place in the national and local newspapers shows him moving from front page news, first as a dazzlingly ingenious fugitive, then as an escaped prisoner able to articulate complaints that chimed with reformist views, to being an occasional feature in the sensationalist Sunday supplements as his self-mutilation and eccentricity made him a figure of voyeuristic fascination. This is echoed by more recent attempts by some notorious prisoners to exploit press and public interest through accounts of their lives that they hope will establish their right to be taken seriously.[12]

Yet, while Perry's record as a campaigning writer may have been one of ultimate failure, certainly to achieve the outcomes he wanted, there is evidence that writing did have more personal benefits. And it is in this private space of writing that the connection between the blind, naked prisoner in 1908 and the prison writers of today, and the value of writing in prison, is most evident.

In Oliver Perry's personal file in the archives of the Dannemora State Hospital are hundreds of notes, letters, 'Bills of Fare', and poems to which I was granted access while researching his life.[13] Prisoners had been extended greater letter writing privileges through the 1890s, although content and frequency was still closely regulated.[14] Perry took full advantage of this, as his file, which includes letters to him as well as his own writing, shows. Some letters are from Amelia Haswell, who wrote to Perry until her death some years before his, one or two are from other inmates who had been released, but most of the letters and all the poems are by Perry. Perry's letters and poems were not, of course, physically written by him because of his blindness; he told reporters that he would give his tobacco ration to other inmates or keepers in return for their services in transcribing his words. The hands range from well-formed copperplate to spider-scrawls, but each letter or poem has a distinctive and rather imposing signature, 'Oliver Curtis Perry': it seems that Perry had practised it before losing his sight and continued to sign his name with a flourish. The 'Bills of Fare', in which he dictated meals that he was prepared to eat, and his many letters make revealing and often entertaining reading; like his earlier interviews, they suggest that his pleasure in words, in stories, and in writing generally, may have held a key to a better life.

If Perry's pleasure in writing was to develop into a practice that could help him do more than pass the time and try to maintain his fragile mental health, it needed to be both encouraged and, ideally, supported. Perry's apparent egotism and history of writing to complain and campaign made his keepers less than sympathetic and the evidence suggests that little was done to foster his creativity in the State Hospitals. Through his relationship with Amelia Haswell, though, the new ideas of the potential benefits of writing for its own sake did reach him and informed his turn to poetry.

Haswell subscribed to the views of Progressive reformers, such as those who inspired and started the *Star of Hope*, that creative activity was not only beneficial as a way of occupying prisoners and deterring them from more troublesome activities but also as a means of helping them, through reflection and creation, to rebuild their lives in preparation for eventual release. She initially encouraged Perry to write as a means to seeking his freedom first through reflecting on his experiences and taking responsibility for his crimes and then by showing this to the world. But while Perry took to poetry with evident pleasure and seems to have reflected on his life and conditions, the desire to use his poetry to persuade the public seems to have been paramount, at least at first. Perry's status as a poet was initially celebrated in the press as yet another facet of a fascinating man. In 1897 a local newspaper noted that this inmate of the local State Hospital was 'something of a poet', and the surviving fragment of the poem it published indicates it was a narrative poem about his life, ending with a defiant verse that was interpreted, with relish, as a possible warning of a future escape:

> I don't intend to serve this out,
> Or even let despair
> Deprive me of my liberty,
> Or give me one grey hair.[15]

A selection of Perry's poems was also published in the *New York Journal* in 1901, with subjects ranging from his father and an unknown 'Sweetheart' to appeals for justice and reform.

The initial press interest in Perry's poetry quickly subsided and did little to add to the impact of his letters and narratives in influencing public opinion, but writing verse seems to have become an ever more important way of maintaining his sense of identity and self-respect. His correspondence reveals the care he took, and difficulties he surmounted, to write at all, and while his letters usually focused on the miseries and wrongs of his situation, his poems reveal other interests and a determination not to become 'DSH 216'. Some of his unpublished poems, like the one submitted to the *Star of Hope*, are explicitly about his situation or are designed to appeal to an individual, such as a new doctor, but others are less obviously 'campaigning' and seem to have been a vital way in which he expressed his feelings in a system that, inadvertently or not, was dehumanising and isolating.

Perry's poetry seems dated now and is rarely exceptional. The forms he uses are conventional and the content sometimes seems banal, but the conditions in which he wrote make such judgments seem inappropriate. His achievement is, in many ways, exceptional. Perry's fondness for, and skill in composing, acrostics, for example, connects with his general pleasure in ingenuity and in being seen to be clever; the man who once used this ingenuity to rob trains, escape from prisons, and to destroy his own sight, eventually used it to make visual impact in poems he would never see. He also shows a rebellious humour in many poems about his conditions and his protests. In a very different Fourth of July poem to the one published in the *Star of Hope*, entitled ‘A Parody’, he reworked the lyrics of the patriotic ‘Marching through Georgia’. One stanza read:

> How the ‘Bugs’ did curse that time, O yes it was a fright;
> How they damned and double-damned the man who’s out of sight;
> How they would have choked me in all my sightless plight
> When I was yelling for freedom.

In his prison file someone has written ‘Illustrative of Perry’s Egotism’ on the poem and while that may be accurate, it is also illustrative of a man making sense of almost unendurable conditions. In this, and other poems, Perry revisits his experiences and holds onto a sense of himself as more than a ‘bug’. This was often to incur the displeasure of his keepers, and most particularly the Superintendent, Dr Charles North.

Dr North had initially appeared to be in tune with a changing prison regime that encouraged good conduct through carefully regulated recreational activities and had started an inmates’ orchestra. Amelia Haswell, encouraged by this, sent Perry a mandolin, as he was fond of music, but, to both her and Perry’s dismay, Dr North would not allow him to keep it. The reason was never given, although Perry’s record of volatile behaviour was the likely cause, but Dr North’s disapproval of Perry’s writing was clearly recorded. In Perry’s file I found two poems that were sealed up in envelopes by Dr North and marked ‘Obscene Verse by Oliver Curtis Perry’. I was allowed to open these envelopes, dated 1900 and 1907, and read their contents. The first, signed ‘July 17th Nineteen Hundred and in love’, was a lyrical, romantic address to an unknown object of Perry’s affection whose acrostic subtext read ‘May I sleep with you’; the other, which had been given to a doctor, was a comical limerick about a young woman doing something very rude indeed with a lily. Read in the context of his life, the fact that Perry could write funny, tricky verse is rather moving, but its censorship connects with a failure on the part of the State Hospital regime to see the potential that writing could have even for a man who had been declared insane.

There is some evidence that the process of creative reflection and composition of writing did have a positive impact on Perry that, in different circumstances, might have helped him to prepare for life beyond the institution. While he was still attempting to influence public opinion about his case, in his later 'life stories' he is less prone to defecting the blame for his situation onto others and romantic embellishments like the dying lover in New Mexico are replaced by reflection on his earlier mistakes and a more realistic hope for his future. By 1917, the twenty-fifth anniversary of his last train robbery, the life story he told a visiting reporter ended with a poignant note that he no longer thought he could prove his sanity but asked to have his sentence reduced so that he could be sent to an asylum as a free man. In the context of his institution and situation even this modest impact on his thinking is a testament to the potential of writing to help inmates reflect on the past and re-imagine the future.

Perry's writing was encouraged by one or two of his physicians and keepers but Dr North's approach to his case seems to have been unusually inflexible. In 1908, near the time when Perry changed his writing identity to 'Mountain Bughouse 216', Amelia Haswell corresponded with Dr North about the disappearance of a book in which Perry had kept copies of his poems. The loss had caused him acute distress and Amelia Haswell clearly felt the need to explain why it mattered: 'I have always encouraged his composing rhyme, as I thought it would help divert his mind [...] If I was blind and had no way of diverting my mind, I am not sure I would have one to divert very long'.[16] The book had been either confiscated as a punishment or stolen by another inmate, but Amelia Haswell was never told what had happened and the book was never returned to Perry.

Perry's isolation increased in the years after this loss and the story of his life, as well as of his lost book, would have no happy ending. His family had never visited him in Dannemora and, although he frequently expressed his longing to see his father, he appeared to have been disowned after being certified. In 1912 Amelia Haswell wrote to his doctors to ask if Perry knew that his father had died in a fall; five years later the woman he called 'mother' died after contracting pneumonia. There is nothing in Perry's file or record to give a clue about his reaction to either death.

His file holds very few documents from the last decade of his life and no examples of writing. Occasional newspaper stories that distorted the near-forgotten outlaw who had killed nobody into 'an insane animal with a terrible lust for blood' ensured that there would be no public support for any campaign for freedom, however limited, and Perry effectively ceased to exist outside the institution.[17] He died on 5 September, 1930, just days before his sixty-fifth birthday after serving thirty-five years of his sentence. His death certificate cites complications after an operation on a hernia and, despite earlier requests to be buried near his sister, who had been murdered at the age of fifteen by her husband at the time of Perry's train robberies, he was buried in the remotest section of the State Hospital graveyard. No sign remains of the stone marker which would simply have read 'DSH 216'.

Writing had not 'worked' in the way that Perry had initially hoped: it did not help him persuade people that he should be freed or that his conditions should be improved.[18] Given his fragile mental health and his context, the extent to which it could work therapeutically, encouraging him to reflect on his past and present and to imagine a better future, was limited. But writing, encouraged by the Christian missionary who applied the ideas of the reform movement to a 'hopeless case', did have a positive impact on Oliver Perry: it helped to relieve the boredom and isolation of his prison and asylum life; it helped to bolster his sense of worth in the worst of conditions, and gave him something to value beyond the desire for material goods that had first brought him to prison.

The scant evidence suggests that in his final years Perry lived a stripped down life where even his book of poems, as a possession, no longer seemed to matter. The last reported interviews with Perry in the years before his death recall him sitting in his cell, wrapped in a blanket, with a bandage over his eyes, reciting his own poetry from memory. In the end, with no chance of a life beyond the institution, Perry escaped into an inner world made better by his writing, and the writing he left behind testifies to a complex and creative man and to the power of words themselves.

Notes

1 My research into Perry's life was conducted in numerous public and private archives. His life and career have been reconstructed through primary sources during several years of research. The sources include prison records, including inmate files with Perry's own correspondence and poetry, at the New York State Archives; the records of each penitentiary under the auspices of the New York Correctional Service; the Pinkerton Detective Agency files at the Library of Congress; and newspapers, census and personal papers. Perry's life, based on that research, is documented in my book *Wanted Man: The Forgotten Story of Oliver Curtis Perry, an American Outlaw* (London and New York: Bloomsbury, 2004). Where references are not given here, sources are identified in *Wanted Man*.

2 Maud Ballington Booth, *After Prison—What?* (New York: H. Revell, 1903). For an account of Booth's place in reform debates see Amy Myrick, 'Escape from the Carceral: Writing by American Prisoners, 1895-1916', *Surveillance & Society*, 2.1 (2004): 93-109.

3 *New York Times*, April 21, 1899. On Warden Sage and the reforms of the period, see Rebecca M. McLennan, *The Crisis of Imprisonment: Protest, Politics, and the Making of the American Penal State, 1776-1941* (Cambridge: Cambridge University Press, 2008), 224-248.

4 See Myrick, 'Escape from the Carceral', 106.

5 *Star of Hope* (Sing Sing, New York State), July 18, 1908 (copy in Perry's Dannemora State Hospital file).

6 See Myrick, 'Escape from the Carceral', 105; McLennan, *The Crisis of Imprisonment*, 224.

7 See Michael Foucault, *Discipline and Punish: The Birth of the Prison* (London: Peregrine, 1979), *passim*.

8 See McLennan, *The Crisis of Imprisonment*, 54 and *passim*.

9 Thomas Mott Osborne, *Within Prison Walls* (New York: Spruce Gulch Press, 1991), 3.

10 Spargo, *Wanted Man*, 1-37.

11 *Utica Saturday Globe*, February, 1917.

12 See, for example, the case of Charles Bronson, whose *Bronson* (London: Blake, 2000) reveals numerous similarities to Perry's case, both in the impact of isolation on mental health and the lure of notoriety, and on the (here fragile) hope offered by creative activity.

13 I would like to record my thanks to the staff at the New York State Archive, Albany, NY and to the New York Department of Corrections for access to prison records.

14 McLennan, *The Crisis of Imprisonment*, 243.

15 *Fishkill Standard*, October, 1897.

16 Letter from Amelia Haswell to Dr Charles North, 1908 (Dannemora State Hospital Records, New York State Archive).

17 Spargo, *Wanted Man*, 230.

18 There is evidence that Perry did influence public and political opinion at the time of his escape in 1895 and persuaded officials to review his case (see Spargo, *Wanted Man, passim.*), but he failed to secure either a return to prison or a commutation of sentence.

Free to Write: Prison Voices

Hannah Priest

THE FIRST PHASE OF the Free to Write project at Liverpool John Moores University ran from 2004-2007. This book, designed for use by prisoners and writers, marks the second phase of the project. Free to Write grew out of conversations between cultural historians and creative writing practitioners within the university, groups of people who shared common interests in the role of writing within the prison system and in the articulation of prison voices both past and present.

While the work of Christian reformers like Elizabeth Fry and Sarah Martin and the rebellious writing career of Oliver Curtis Perry are distanced from contemporary creative writing practice by time, social mores and policy, the issues raised by these historical cases find their echo in some of today's debates about prisoners' writing. The initial intention of the Free to Write project was to advance understanding of the rehabilitation of inmates and recidivism within the penal system, as well as to produce educational resources and outlets for prisoner expression; in this respect, the project belongs to a broader movement over the past century, which has sought to use creative writing (and the arts in general) as more than simply a pastime to remedy idleness or an occupation intended to prevent dissolute behaviour.

Throughout the twentieth century, prisoners' access to writing and publication has been varied, to say the least. In the early half of the century, denial or confiscation of writing materials was common in a number of institutions. While the legacy of earlier reformers was still felt, particularly as regards reading habits and literacy, prisoners were not always encouraged towards any creative endeavours of their own.

While no doubt many prisoners at this time managed to write—letters, poems or memoirs—few examples of prison writing were published and shared with members of society outside prison walls. There were, of course, exceptions to this, and one notable example, W.F.R. Macartney's autobiographical account of life in Parkhurst entitled *Walls Have Mouths* (1936), implied a relationship between the way prisoners are perceived and a denial of prisoners' writing. Macartney wrote that 'the convict is treated unnaturally: he [...] must not speak'.[1]

As can be seen from the title of his memoir, as well as from its contents, Macartney felt that there was something inherently wrong with this closing of prisoners' 'mouths'. His writing was an act of speech, an act of regaining his own voice and asking others to listen to it.

In many ways, Macartney's memoir reminds us of the story of Oliver Perry, whose earlier writings can be interpreted as an act of 'speaking out' against the situation and conditions in which he found himself. However, it is also important to note that Macartney's autobiography—though now long out of print—did find a publisher outside the prison walls. It was (and, by those who are able to obtain a copy, is) read by members of the public who perhaps would never set foot inside a prison. It is works like *Walls Have Mouths*—and the other early twentieth-century prison memoirs that saw the light on the other side of the wall—that begin to bridge the gap between historical cases and contemporary practice and policy.

Historical instances of prisoner writing raise some important questions for a contemporary creative writing project. Why is freedom to write necessary for prisoners? How does this benefit someone within the prison system? How can a prisoner's 'voice' help their rehabilitation? And how will this benefit society as a whole? Understanding the answers to these questions has been of central concern to prisoner writing projects from the 1960s onwards, as they were—though perhaps expressed somewhat differently—for earlier prison reformers and educators.

In 1962 Arthur Koestler founded an award scheme for prisoner writing and artwork. Originally planned as an award for essay writing, the Koestler awards were intended to reward creative, productive activity. Himself a former political prisoner, Koestler was a firm believer in the positive impact of mental stimulation on a prisoner's wellbeing and rehabilitation. He viewed boredom as the main 'enemy' of the prisoner, and he predicted that counteracting this would become even more vital when (as he rightly anticipated) the abolition of the death penalty lead to an increase in prisoners serving life-tariffs.[2] Koestler's championing of intellectual activity for prisoners is reminiscent of the work of prison reformers Elizabeth Fry and Sarah Martin: stimulation of the mind and the pursuit of 'higher' things are encouraged as a way to transcend both the reality of imprisonment and the circumstances which may have led to it.

However, while Koestler's original focus was intellectual and academic stimulation, his legacy is somewhat broader. At the time of writing, the Koestler award scheme has just passed its fiftieth birthday and now offers awards for work in the visual arts and creative writing, as well as mentor programmes, exhibitions and sale of prisoner art. Like many organisations working in this field, the Koestler Trust recognise and promote the need for prisoner *creativity*—beyond mental stimulation or productivity—as a means of recovery, rehabilitation and understanding.

Arthur Koestler's work was one of a number of attempts made in the second half of the twentieth century to identify and develop creative expression in prisons. His was a unique intervention, with a lasting legacy; however, it was also part of a wider move towards offering creative expression—particularly, for the interests of this essay, creative writing—as an option open to all prisoners. By the 1970s, the therapeutic benefits of prisoner life-writing were beginning to be recognised. In his history of British prison writing, Julian Broadhead notes that, unlike many earlier autobiographers, Jimmy Boyle was able to write *A Sense of Freedom* (1977) 'without hindrance or concern that his manuscript would be confiscated' during his time in the Barlinnie Special Unit.[3] Just under a decade later, the UK prison system's first writer-in-residence, Tom Hadaway, took up a post at HMP Durham, a placement co-funded by the WRVS, Northern Arts and the Arts Council.[4]

The introduction of a writer-in-residence to a prison signalled a clear recognition of creativity as a beneficial practice for prisoners, prisons and the wider public. While education services provided—and continue to provide—valuable literacy and reading skills, a writer in a prison offers something rather different. Writer-in-residence programmes developed further in the years following Hadaway's appointment, with the Writers in Residence in Prison Scheme being set up in 1992 by the Arts Council of England and the Home Office to offer placements for writers in various institutions throughout the United Kingdom. In 1998, the Writers in Prisons Network was appointed by the Arts Council to administer this scheme in recognition of the 'ongoing needs of prisons, writers and inmates involved in residencies'.[5]

In addition to longer-term residencies offered by the Writers in Prisons Network, a number of arts organisations have run shorter, focused projects in prisons and young offender institutions. For example, in 2006-7, Apples and Snakes co-ordinated the Inside Out project in Greater Manchester. Amongst the short-term residencies that formed this project were a workshop course led by Mike Garry and Diké Omeje at HMPYOI Hindley and weekly poetry sessions at HMPYOI Styal led by Ali Gadema and Chanje Kunda. All the poets involved in the project mentored prisoners in creative writing, but also led reading groups and performance workshops.[6]

The past couple of decades have seen an increase in the number of creative professionals working in prisons, but also a dramatic increase in the number of outlets for publication and performance of prisoners' creative writing. It is certainly true that, for as long as there have been prisons, there have been writers producing work within their walls: Thomas Malory's *Morte Darthur* may be one of the earliest examples, but John Bunyon's *The Pilgrim's Progress* and Oscar Wilde's *De*

Profundis are perhaps more well-known as seminal works of English Literature produced inside a prison.[7] A number of prison memoirs were published during the twentieth century, the number dramatically increasing in the later decades, although it should be noted that the majority of these were published after the writer's release. However, interest in and outlets for poetry, fiction and other creative writing by those still within the prison system were (and, to an extent, still are) limited. An important aspect of many twenty-first century projects is the dissemination of prisoners' work, either through print publication or performance.

Prisoners' access to publication is a legal, moral and practical battleground, with equally vocal challengers and supporters. For every high-profile case of an individual publishing and profiting from work produced while serving a sentence—for example, Jeffrey Archer's publication of his *Prison Diaries*—there is an equally high-profile case of a prisoner being denied the opportunity to release autobiographical material—as in the High Court's ruling that the confiscation of Denis Nilsen's autobiography by staff at HMP Full Sutton must stand to prevent Nilsen's intended publication of the book.

Nevertheless, a significant number of contemporary writing projects have worked with publication as an ultimate goal and a number of anthologies of prisoner writing have been produced as a result. Indeed, the Free to Write collection itself is one such anthology, including as it does examples of creative writing written in UK prisons. In addition to this, local magazines produced for and by prisoners in individual institutions have been encouraged and supported by writers-in-residence and education staff, and national magazines such as *Inside Time* and *Women in Prison* offer further avenues for publication of creative writing and letters. Considering the intended impact and benefit of such outlets reveals an awareness of the rehabilitative and reflective potency of creative expression, but also significant connection with much earlier publications such as the American journal *Star of Hope*.

As seen in the quote above from Macartney's 1936 autobiography, supporters of prisoners' right to write have long considered the suppression of prisoners' voices to be 'unnatural'. Contemporary practitioners speak of the power of creative writing to 'rehumanise' and 'reconnect' a prisoner with his or her community.[8] This is also of concern to projects working with individuals on release. For instance, as part of the Free to Write project, a writers' group was established at Adelaide House, an all-female bail hostel in Liverpool, leading to the production of a magazine (*Adeladies*). In her foreword to one issue, Jenny Newman states that the magazine 'aims at introducing its authors to the rest of the community. [...] All [the writers] are united in their desire to create a better future for themselves, and to make a contribution to community living.'[9]

For some, creative writing has a unique role to play in this 'reconnection'. Broadhead describes writing as a means through which an individual can 'clarify the past',[10] and this is echoed in the reflective nature of many writing exercises, particular those involving life-writing. However, he also states that 'writing is often more of a confrontational experience', which can differentiate it from the 'escape for the artist' found in other media.[11] Writing, then, requires a more forthright engagement with past crimes, present circumstances and, significantly, with future potential.

Former Youth Offender Team worker, playwright and writer-in-residence at HMYOI Lancaster Farms Michael Crowley makes a powerful claim for the rehabilitative power of artistic expression in the editor's note to an anthology of writing produced by young offenders at Lancaster Farms. He states that:

> Crime is often about pursuing short cuts, chasing maximum reward through minimum effort. [...] Art asks for the maximum degree of effort and gives no certainty of any reward. Art is the opposite of crime. That is why, for rehabilitative purposes, it is important that prisoners are presented with the opportunity to paint, dance and especially write.[12]

For Crowley, the purpose of creative writing work with young offenders is to rehabilitate and reduce the risk of reoffending. By offering writing and publication as an 'opportunity', the writer-in-residence encourages offenders towards the 'opposite of crime', the path of 'maximum degree of effort' and 'no certainty of any reward'.

Broadhead's idea of clarification of the past and confrontational experience—like Crowley's recognition of the importance of asking 'for the maximum degree of effort'—identifies the role creative writing might play in a prisoner's personal development. Whether in relation to remorse, understanding of past behaviour or the avoidance of future crime, creative writing programmes and workshops are often part of an individual's rehabilitation. In some cases, writing has taken on a more tangible role, offering a future career for some released prisoners. A number of individuals who benefitted from creating writing whilst serving a sentence have gone on to earn a living from writing, teaching or mentoring. For instance, Anna Reynolds, the first editor of *Inside Time*, began writing while serving a life sentence for murder. Since her sentence was quashed, Reynolds has enjoyed a career as a novelist and playwright as well as editing the national prisoners' newspaper. In the 1990s Reynolds also worked as a writer-in-residence at HMP Holloway and HMP Bedford.

However, the role of writing in fostering 'connection' and 'community' is not just valued in terms of individual rehabilitation. Like the early twentieth-century *Star of Hope*, many creative writing projects today focus on the significance of prisoner writing for other prisoners. Publication of work is often disseminated first and foremost within the prison system. For some practitioners, this is used as a way of increasing engagement with reading and writing programmes: 'authenticity' of voice and experience being, perhaps, more compelling material. A number of projects have sought to use prisoners' writing as a means of helping new or young prisoners come to terms with the reality of their circumstances, with life-writing, poetry and prose being used as tools for providing advice and mentoring. Internal prisoner-authored newspapers—like, for example, *Roast*, the newspaper run by inmates at HMYOI Glen Parva during Gareth Creer's writer-residency—can be valuable sources of practical information, encouragement, sympathy and solidarity.

In some cases, it has been suggested that simply the opportunity to read work by another prisoner—or to know that one's words are being read by another—can be beneficial in itself. In commenting on creative writing workshops held at HMP Bronzefield, poet Leah Thorn states: 'Many of the women said that writing helps them to deal with their emotions and that reading other women's words help them feel less alone.'[13]

Thorn's words about the workshops at HMP Bronzefield are a reminder of the importance of 'voice' for marginalised groups within the prison system. In recent years, work with young offenders, female prisoners and BME prisoners has sought to address the multiple issues faced by inmates, and the ways in which writing can be used to navigate intersecting problems of social identity, a sense of hopelessness and external pressure. Again, the focus of such work is often on rehabilitation, but for many projects—on the inside as on the outside—giving 'voice' to the 'voiceless' is seen as a valuable end in itself.

The Seeds of Forgiveness project at HMP Downview is an example of such practice. This creative writing project led to the publication of an anthology of female prisoners' poetry, which revealed the complexity of a notion of 'forgiveness' for women within the prison system. Inmates were encouraged to use poetry to explore their personal relationships with 'forgiveness'; while some wrote about the possibilities for being forgiven, others wrote of their need to forgive abusers.[14] Similarly, projects have been run to use writing as a tool to understand and examine issues faced by BME prisoners in the UK. In 2001 Apples and Snakes received funding from the Paul Hamlyn Foundation to run a Black History Month project in HMP Wandsworth, and have since worked with Segun Lee-French (on the 2011 Poetic Licence project), a poet with several years' experience of running workshops for the Partners of Prisoners' Black Prisoner Support Group.[15] These various projects reveal a concern with 'connection' and 'community', as well as with the vital roles history, relationships and support play in a prisoners' wellbeing and development.

There is a final aspect of prisoner writing that is important to address—one which has relevance to the *Free to Write* anthology as well as many of the projects discussed above. Publication and dissemination of prisoners' work is not always limited to intra- and inter-prison circulation: some anthologies, magazines and books are intended for a wider audience, and are available to members of the public outside the prison system. The annual Koestler Trust exhibition now attracts around 30,000 visitors a year, and their anthologies of prize-winning poetry and prose are easily available to the non-prison population. Clearly, organisations such as the Koestler Trust have a firm belief in the benefits of circulating work from inside amongst those on the outside.

Throughout the history of prison writing—which is also the history of prisons—memoirs and life-writing have been used as tools of reform. Or, if not reform *per se*, public education about the reality and conditions of prisons. As can be seen in the story of Oliver Perry, poetry and letter writing have long been utilised by prisoners determined to bring their circumstances to the attention of a wider audience and, in some cases, to attempt to effect change. While the majority of contemporary writing projects have rehabilitation, remorse and recidivism as their primary points of concern, the role of writing in societal, rather than individual, reform has not been entirely abandoned. Both *Inside Time* and *Women in Prison*—publications circulated throughout the prison system—have letters pages in which prisoners can voice their concerns (and complaints). One example of such a letter, from 2010, reveals the continuing relationship between letter-writing, reform and poetry. Pammy Clarke (New Hall Prison) writes asking for consideration to be given to gay women prisoners and their separation from partners/wives while in jail. The letter is brief and ends with a poem, 'written from the heart for all women in jail in love', entitled 'Segregated Love'.[16] While this poem perhaps lacks the confrontational force of the 1908 submission to the *Star of Hope* by 'Mountain Bughouse 216', it is an important reminder of the continuing power (or hope) of poetry to bring about change and articulate frustration.

Prisoner writing is also offered as a means through which society's views of imprisonment and imprisoned individuals can be confronted and, potentially, changed. In 1995 Clive Hopwood of the (now) Writers in Prisons Network wrote of the need to address public perceptions of prisoners, and the role that creative writing might play in this:

> We hear little in the media of the prisoner's voice—they have no right to be heard, they're criminals—but perhaps if we listened a little more to what they have to say... about drugs, violence, crime, the justice system, the prisons, about what matters to them... perhaps we might understand a little better and judge more wisely.[17]

Hopwood is not alone in advocating understanding and 'wiser' judgement. For others, the role of 'rehumanising' the prisoner through creative writing is also one of 'rehumanising' society's response to those within the prison system through the circulation of prisoners' work. Caspar Walsh, a writer with varied experience of the prison system (as a visitor, an inmate, a writer-in-residence and a workshop leader), includes a quote from Fyodor Dostoevsky on his website, which encapsulates his approach to prisoner writing projects: 'A society should not be judged by how it treats its outstanding citizens but by how it treats its criminals.'[18]

In conclusion, I would like to offer a further quote from a prison writer-in-residence on the role of writing in prisons. In the introduction to *Parc Prison—Released*, Graham Hartill writes of the work produced as part of organised writing programmes, but he also acknowledges the fact that prisoner creativity is not limited to 'sanctioned' or formal sessions. On the inside—as on the outside—creative endeavour can be a spontaneous response to circumstance, a personal experience and an individual form of expression: 'there is writing—and talking—back in the cells, shown—or rapped—to friends, that staff like me will never see or hear: it isn't meant for us, and doesn't demand our approval'.[19] Hartill's comment here reminds us that writing in prisons, in fact, has much in common with writing outside prisons. If we view the latter as having benefit, then the former must also. It also serves as an assertion of the significance of creativity for the individual, and the need to acknowledge that while those on the outside may 'never see or hear' the work that 'doesn't demand [their] approval', creativity amongst prisoners is an undeniable reality. Contemporary projects have sought to expand the platform for this creativity, and bring its reality to a wider audience.

This essay has deliberately concentrated on the recent history of creative writing in prisons and the views from 'outside' on its benefits, functions and purpose. The intention was to examine some of the points of comparison and divergence from the historical cases explored in the earlier essays. However, *Free to Write* has a dual purpose, and this essay also serves as an introduction to the writing that will be showcased in the book's second section. The Free to Write project is situated within a history of acknowledging and identifying prisoners' voices through creative writing. As such, it is appropriate that the subsequent section of this book offers a contemporary selection of these voices.

Notes

1 W.F.R. Macartney, *Walls Have Mouths* (1936), cited in Julian Broadhead, *Unlocking the Prison Muse: The Inspirations and Effects of Prisoners' Writing in Britain* (Cambridge: Cambridge Academic, 2006), 12.
2 I am grateful to Tim Robertson, Chief Executive of the Koestler Trust, for his valuable assistance with regards to Arthur Koestler's work and legacy. See also Michael Scammell, *Koestler: The Indispensable Intellectual* (London: Faber and Faber, 2009).
3 Broadhead, *Unlocking the Prison Muse*, 24.
4 *Ibid.*, 120.
5 Quote taken from the Writers in Prisons Network's 'Introduction for Writers' document (April, 1999). I am grateful to Clive Hopwood of the WIPN for his assistance with regards to the history of the Writers in Residence in Prison Scheme.
6 I would like to thank Nicky Crabb at Apples and Snakes and the poets involved, particularly Tony Walsh, for providing detailed information about the Inside Out project.
7 While Oscar Wilde's *The Ballad of Reading Gaol* is better known, and was certainly inspired by events that took place during the writer's incarceration, it was in fact written after he was released in 1897.
8 These terms were used in various correspondence with Joy Winkler, Tony Walsh, John Siddique and Ben Mellor, all of whom have completed residences with WIPN or Apples and Snakes.
9 Jenny Newman, 'Foreword', in *Adeladies* (2004): 3.
10 Broadhead, *Unlocking the Prison Muse*, 111.
11 *Ibid.*, 168.
12 Michael Crowley, 'Editor's Note', in *Time of Death: Fiction, Poetry and Memoir From HM YOI Lancaster Farms* (2012), 1.
13 Leah Thorn, quoted in *Women in Prison* (Summer, 2010): 31.
14 See *Women in Prison*, 40-43.
15 Again, I am grateful to Nicky Crabb of Apples and Snakes for providing background information on the Poetic Licence project.
16 *Women in Prison*, 48.
17 Clive Hopwood, 'Foreword', in *All Men are Equalish: The View From Inside Prison (HMP Swansea)* (Clwyd: I*D Books, 1995), 7.
18 See http://www.casparwalsh.co.uk/workshops/prison-work.html. I am grateful to Caspar Walsh for personal communication explaining the significance of this quote and its relationship to the work he has done with in prisons and young offenders institutions.
19 Graham Hartill, 'Introduction', in *Parc Prison—Released* (Bedlinog, 2010), 1.

Prison Voices: Present

Commentary by Adam Creed

THIS COLLECTION OF prison writing contains poems, short stories and autobiography, but every piece is a story. We are all living our own stories and all stories have a beginning, a middle and an end. So has this story: the story of why putting a pen to paper, why just even thinking about your own story, can help you write a better ending for yourself.

There are three types of prison writing:

1. Writing that tries to make sense of what made us who we are, to unravel what brought us to here, now. This is descriptive writing, unearthing something about ourselves.

2. There's writing which comes to terms with the situation we are in now. What are we going to do about it? How will we get through? Arranging our thoughts about where we are now can help us cope. There might be a sense of injustice or there might be a sense of remorse, for the ills we have suffered or inflicted. This is analytical writing.

3. There's writing your way out. Taking the first and second of what went before and imagining a different ending. What will happen on the out? Relationships, family, housing and work. What do we love about life and what are the dangers? What path to design and follow? Maybe putting pen to paper can help us see what's really important. This is aspirational writing.

Read on and hear what others in your situation have thought and remembered and plotted for themselves. That's the beauty of words: they give us a window into the lives of others.

Beginnings

In these stories, the writers describe what it is to be free. It is a precarious and almost unnatural state. These writers all describe being on the cusp of a change, and muse upon what it is to be guilty. Jon H makes us feel free under the hot sun, but there's an overwhelming sense that we are coming to the end of an age of innocence, and in 'My Left Eye' John H shows how we can sometimes feel separate from the things we do. There is tremendous humour in his contemplation of guilt and innocence. 'Meeting Tim' lays bare the things that make us what we are, the raw materials of people born and raised in unfortunate circumstances, and in Stuart's joyous 'Just an Egg' he is saved from a life of crime by a love of the natural world. We need faith to do the right things, but that faith is a frail thing and if it is damaged, we can easily go the wrong way.

My Left Eye

John H (HMP Shrewsbury)

My left eye is a wonderful thing.
It has a life of its own.
It stopped being mine when I was only four.
Now it thinks it's self-employed.
It's less obedient than a deaf dog,
But it gets just as excited
When it sees something it likes,
And it's off! And I can't do a thing.
I have been in trouble with it once or twice,
As you can probably imagine.
It's quite funny to see
The person I am talking to
Look over their shoulder suddenly
To see what my eye has found;
Or on a long car journey,

The person sat next to me asks,
Why are you staring at me?
I explain that my eye is not mine,
But they never believe me.
So I do apologise in advance,
If my left eye takes a fancy to you.

The Best Summer Ever!

Jon H (HMP Frankland)

A warm summer breeze drifts lazily across meticulously manicured gardens. The pungent smell of freshly cut grass fills my nostrils. I smile to myself. The distant hum of a lawn mower rings gently in my ears. I love the summer. Slowly, I lift my head, not wanting to do anything too quickly. It feels like a gargantuan effort, the heat of the sun presses down on me like hot bonds pulling me back onto the cool comforting grass. I lose the will to get up. Another five minutes will not hurt, I think to myself.

1976, the year Great Britain had one of the most amazing summer heat waves. I was nine years old, only one year away from the illustrious ten! I was almost grown up, or so I thought. Most of that summer was spent enjoying the weather, having my first girlfriend and getting my heart broken. What a summer to be nine!

This was the year I learned the joy of sunbathing. I had just been bought my first transistor radio by my grandfather. I would sit in our garden and listen to Radio 1 for hours on end. I was one of those lucky people who did not get sunburn, so I could sunbathe all day, and not get burnt, much to the envy of others who could not.

I met my first girlfriend that summer. She was in my class at school and we were already good friends, we hung out in the same group too. She was the same age as me and we thought we were in love. I was so happy and thought that this was how life would always be.

In the early evenings all my brother and sister's friends would descend on our house for a game of two man hunt or kick the can. This was because we had a large enough garden for everyone to be able to hide. There could be upwards of twenty youngsters running around our garden every evening, shouts of triumph occasionally being heard as the last of a hiding party was found. I loved getting involved in these games. Bedtime was always a sad affair as I did not want to stop the fun.

Mornings for me meant padding round our garden barefoot. I would often look for new places to hide or just explore as I loved to do.

The afternoons were a magical time as my girlfriend and I would skulk off somewhere quiet for a snog, or we would play in our garden away from everyone else. Sometimes a few of my friends and I would laze around in the graveyard next to my dad's church. It was far enough away from the adults for those who had girlfriends to get a snog in peace and quiet. This was to be my undoing, as my girlfriend was to be poached by an older boy later that summer. A group of older children joined our group in the graveyard and we started smoking and playing games like kiss-chase and dare. This was when I discovered my girlfriend kissing another boy. I did not play outside my garden for about a week after that. We made friends again and I got over it, but it was never the same. I saw the downside to having a girlfriend.

As this long hot summer drew to a close, I became aware that I had grown older, a little wiser and more street smart to the ways of the world. I had started to explore further afield and discovered new places to hang out and sunbathe, or just sit and wonder.

I found another church just down the road from where we lived. At the back were the most beautiful gardens, they were so well kept and I thought it was a representation of heaven on earth. This was to become my new hangout place. Often I would go alone and just lie in the sun and enjoy the sounds of summer's breeze drifting to my ears. The scent of roses invaded my nostrils and gave me a sense of euphoria and tranquillity. Often I found myself just marvelling at the beauty of the flower beds and their amazing scents. I did introduce one or two friends to this paradise, but for the most part, I preferred to keep it to myself.

Summer turned to autumn. The school term was about to begin. Life began to pick up pace. I began to wonder what next summer would be like.

Meeting Tim

Anonymous (HMP Lancaster Farms)

I buried my feelings. I didn't want you to know how important this was to me. I didn't want you to see the anger inside of me, lying dormant like a bear in midwinter, for not being there all those years, what you did to my mum by not rescuing me that night. So when I met you I stood waiting with my hood up. Thirteen years since I'd last seen you. Thirteen years since you'd gambled with my life. A man pulls up on the kerb and looks at me with my sister's eyes. That face, alien but familiar, like a photo of the people who used to be family in another lifetime. My granddad: a fictional character with my eyes who smiles back at me as I look through the pictures I keep under my bed. He looks like me so he must be real. He's out there somewhere. I used to think about you like that. Now you're a real person standing in front of me. What do I know about you? All I know is that you've been to prison. We find ourselves on perverse common ground. We've both done time and at least we have something to talk about. You're small in stature with a big presence. Them blue eyes with a touch of menace stare straight through me. You stand at a distance. We size each other up, both of us wary, both of us willing one another to make the first move. Father and son both at a crossroads: me, *should I spark him or hug him?* You, *if I go to hug him, will he reject me?*

Then you say, 'Alright son?'

'What's going on dad?'

Then you hug me. I feel relieved. It was like I was home. The fragmented pieces of my life were beginning to take shape. It was like a jigsaw and you were the first big piece sending me on the road to understanding my life and family. Now that you are back I'm prepared to forgive but not forget. I don't want to lose you again. So some things are best left unsaid, but you know what you did that night thirteen years ago when you left me to die in that fire.

Just an Egg

Stuart (HMP Greenock)

When I was thirteen years old I had a fascination for wild birds and their eggs. I used to travel all over collecting birds eggs until one day at Castle Semple loch in Lochwinnoch (an RSPB reserve) my friend and I hired canoes to get to the water birds' nests that we couldn't reach from the land.

Unfortunately, we were spotted and when we came back to dry land we were arrested. The wardens were lying in wait for us and we were taken to a big building with our haul of eggs. We had raided the common-gull colony, the mute swan's nest and we also had eider teal and tufted ducks' eggs. We had over sixty eggs between us but the eggs that caused the problems for us were the four dirty grey eggs of a bird called the little grebe, sometimes known as the dabchick, one of only seventeen breeding pairs in the country.

This was in 1975 and we were young, so instead of phoning the police they placed us in a jeep and drove us to a large wooden building, one of the wardens watching over us. Soon a projector and a large roll of film were produced and we were told to watch a film of these birds taken the year before. Instead of my normal view of birds fleeing in panic as I raided their nests, I was watching a film of grebes dancing with each other on the water. I saw the male grebe present the female with a piece of water reed, which was her first piece of nesting material. I watched as the birds worked nonstop to build their nest and guard their eggs from hungry gulls. Then the glorious day mum appeared with the little grey heads of the chicks looking cute from between the wings on her back as she swam. Finally we watched the chicks fledging and flying away.

The lights went on and Gary the warden asked, 'How do you feel now?' I hung my head in shame. To me it was only the shell that had the interest—the sizes, the colours, the squiggles and spots on them. My days of egg collecting were over. The birds were better to watch.

I got a voluntary job with Gary on Castle Semple loch, until I was sixteen, then a full-time job with the RSPB. I went to Skomer Island in

North Wales one March, to see how the puffins were coping due to overfishing and to ring the young birds. These comical birds nested in burrows on the island which was about half a mile wide and was covered with old, unused burrows. I asked John and Susan (my companions) how it was possible to find the burrows the birds were using. They both looked at me. Smiling, Susan said, 'You'll find out tonight.'

Finally midnight came. I carried what can best be described as a bag full of knitting needles with plastic flags attached at the blunt end. After ten minutes walking in the dark John and Susan stopped at a grassy hill. Treading quietly, they knelt down at burrow after burrow. Suddenly Susan motioned for me to kneel down beside her at a particular burrow. I knelt down, put my ear to the burrow and started to laugh. Those little birds snored! A flag was pushed into the ground to mark the spot and the hunt continued. We found seventy-four of those birds snoring in their nest tunnels. Looking at an egg had never amazed me like this.

For the next five years I worked all over the British Isles with the RSPB. In 1990 I was sent to Loch Garten to monitor the only breeding pair of ospreys the public knew about in the country. I was there about a month when we had a phone call saying a young peregrine falcon had been struck by a car. The driver stated he had placed the bird in the phone box he was calling from (as it had attacked him with its talons while he was driving); he gave us directions and told us he would meet us there. Looking at the map we realised it was on a small highland road over twelve miles away. We made our way over there but there was no sign of a phone box anywhere. After two hours we made our way back to the ospreys and to my horror I realised the tree containing the ospreys nest had been cut down. I had watched as the birds had returned from Africa to rebuild their nest, the female incubate the eggs for three weeks and now they lay smashed at my feet. That day I realised how that warden had felt in Lochwinnoch. It wasn't just an egg; it was a life.

I gave my job up soon after that as I couldn't understand why I was so upset about a nest. That bird lost its young that year. Me, I've been in and out of jail ever since and racked up over twenty years in sentences. It turns out not only those young birds lost their lives that year.

The Middle: Reflections and Awareness

There is no shortage of time when you are in prison, so writing can be a productive means of channelling thoughts and structuring plans for the future. In the stories that follow, the writers reflect upon their situation, analysing the state of their lives, thinking about what turn their own stories might take. As with all stories, the middle of a story is where we consider the motives for our behaviour and the consequences of our actions. If the beginning is The Life Before, this part of the collection is The Life Inside. Often, if a person can look deeply into where they are and what sequence of actions brought them to this place, they might also see beyond the inevitability of re-offending.

At the very least, the process of writing can make us feel good about ourselves. As the artist and ex-offender, Frank Cook, says:

> With the encouragement of other people I became braver and stronger and began to love myself because I had accomplished something that I thought only good, intelligent people did. Previously I thought that because I was a criminal I could never be like them but now I am... and it started from an art class.

Prison writing can educate people on the outside as to what life in prison is really like. Prison writing can show people the full story as to why and how people end up in jail and in this way it is has a role to play in penal reform, by showing the complexities of the causes of crime and the difficulties within the process of rehabilitation. It brings to life what academics call the 'variable reality of imprisonment'. Every inmate is an individual with their own set of circumstances which delivered them to this place.

So, we learn a little of what it is to be a number, and that sense of identity is also explored by Ryan who makes sense of his past. In 'Red by Colour, Red by Nature' we get a prisoner's take on how nobody should be above the law. 'Chicken Madras in Wythenshawe' paints a picture of the greyness of prison life. In 'The Coodgie', Lindsay describes prison life from a distance, symbolising a 'coodgie' and showing that some things are the same inside or out, and Cathy R's story reveals that we all have a goodness waiting to be discovered, a theme also developed by Richie D.

Untitled

Anonymous

In prison you're given a number. My number is 98060, but that's not who I am. My name is less important than my number. It was when I was listening to music and thinking about how often I'm asked what my number is that I was inspired to write these lyrics. When I get my canteen—what's your number? When I go to a visit—what's your number? When I pick up my mail—what's your number? When I'm walking on the route—what's your number? When I'm at education—when I get my medication—what's your number? They built a new prison recently which is where I've been serving my sentence and they made space for 700 more numbers like me. It seems like the more room they create the more numbers they make. When you're outside you have another chance to be who you really are. When I'm outside I'm John.

The Day I Left Home

Ryan (HMP Lancaster Farms)

Is that the time already? Got to be making tracks. It's raining, which is to be expected on a day like this. 2nd September, I'm sixteen in twenty days. I'll roll a spliff and get off. Where did I put the rizlas? I'll have to wait until I get to DJ's gaff. Make my room tidy before I go. Why bother though? I'm not coming back. Still you have to have respect. Grab my phone, pull on my jacket, slip on my trainers, open my safe and grab my dough (that won't last long), throw all my life essentials into two holdalls. I carry them downstairs and stop at the door to write a note. *What should I write?* This is pressure. Sit down on the stairs, finish my cig, pick up the pen. *Dad I can't stay here no more. I need my own place. Call you soon. Ryan.* That was a lie. Call you soon? Yeah in a month or two. Open the front door, lock it behind me, post the key through the front letterbox, make tracks. Turn right down the back path onto the estate, go to DJ's gaff.

'Alright Mrs James.'

Got a lot of respect for DJ's mum.

'Hiya Ryan. So you finally left. What's your dad gonna say?'

'I don't know. Probably get on the phone. Start chatting shit. Flipping out.'

'You shouldn't speak about your dad like that—'

Mrs James giving me another lecture—I've heard it all before. One p.m. Who's this calling? DJ's got the shots lined up. It's Dad and I can't be arsed with this.

'So you finally left then? Why don't you come back and we'll talk it through?'

'Fuck that, Dad. We don't need to talk.'

'Okay then, but I just wanted to chat.'

Wait a minute. Why isn't he flipping out? Maybe I broke the last straw, maybe he's tired of arguing, maybe he's past anger and just feels regret, maybe his heart is broken.

'But I don't want to talk, Dad.'

'Have you got money son? If you need any—'

'I don't want anything off you.'

'Alright I guess this is it. One last thing—if you carry on like you are, you're going to be in jail by the time you're eighteen.'

'Don't try preaching to me.'

I put the phone down. He was wrong. I was in jail by the time I was seventeen.

Red by Colour, Red by Nature

On seeing a picture of Rebekah Brookes close to one of a red-robed nun looking after a starving child

Nick C (HMP Shrewsbury)

Red is the robe that holds a life
Red is the hair that distracts from the truth
Red is the blood that is too weak to bleed
Red is the headline hewn from tabloid rock
Red is the colour drawn on the map
Red is the Fox who delivers the news
Red are the eyes, burned with sorrow
Red is the Sky, shrouded in mist
Red is the dust, just blowin' in the wind
Red is the anger that bellows within
Red is the cross that has no frontiers
Red are the faces, blushed with regret
Red is the soil where the bodies are laid
Red are our leaders' submissive hands
Red are the guns that militias play tunes on
Red are the phones, hacked to death
Red tops think they can take us for fools
Red is the line that cannot be crossed.

Chicken Madras in Wythenshawe

James (HMP Lancaster Farms)

Mango chutney and red onions
That's what triggers it
It gets my taste buds watering
Just thinking about it
Just thinking about you

The smell of paint when we moved in together
That new brown carpet
The sound of racing party music
The touch of your hair your calf
Sitting behind you on a blue motorbike
Your tanned skin your faith in me
Your hand in my hand in the hospital
My dreams about the pink bedroom

Having a bath together and
Taking photos with our phones
Running round after the dog
Cleaning the mess up
Your brown hair your belief
All these things I still have
Always and forever

Graffiti

Richie D (HMP Frankland)

Dust seeps out seeking the cold night air
Tap tap—those footsteps clash the desert-like ground
creating mists of dirt sprinkling without a sound
worn soles without a doubt
these shoes have trod on foreign ground and forbidden places
that only the brave dare to leave their mark.

People call us degenerates, vandals who should be locked away
criminals who deface buildings, street corners, shops with those pretty steel shutters,
trains, planes, vans and billboards.
I could go on but you get my meaning.
It's not that we are degenerate defacing vandals out to commit crimes,
it's that we are every one of you who has a dream
and who wants to share our dreams with others
who need to tell a story, their story as yours:

We are the forgotten
We are your children

We are the streets and life that breathes it.
Questions, answers, hope, understanding.
Fear we bring to these streets.
Art is not a game,
It's life!

The Coodgie

Lindsay H

Thursday efternoon again, canteen day, the Coodgies are stakin oot their prey already. Like hawks aboot tae swoop in fur the kill. Canteen's a special day oot the week fur the Coodgie. They know fur sure this is wan day oot the week when ye cannae say 'Ah've no goat any.' Canteen bags get dished oot, straight away there's a Coodgie in yer Peter. 'Awright mate?' his wee beady eyes ur scanning yer full hoose, the hale time his mooth dribbles the usual pish. He's already goat an empty cup in his haund (who walks aboot wi an empty cup?—the Coodgies dae!) He spots the canteen bag that ye've tried haurd tae shift right under yer bunk. He's in a quandary noo. He's come here under the guise ae exchanging pleasantries wae ye, but the underlying motive ae his wait is tae ask ye for summit afore movin oan tae his next victim.

Noo he's clocked yer canteen bag an he cannae make up his mind whit he wants tae cadge. There's a coupla different types a Coodgie. Ye've goat the 'poor wee me' Coodgie, that wid huv ye believe he's goat the weight a the world oan his shooders. He disnae care whit ye think aboot his beggin antics, he'll jist blantantly ask ye fur anything that he's no goat: yer supposed tae understaun his predicament. Noo the other Coodgie, he's an experienced character, his full week, 24 hoors a day ur aw worked oot. Jist lik a real joab. This guy is skillfull wi his people skills, his patter, an ability tae adapt any situation tae his advantage. Integratin hisel intae company an ay leavin the table wi summit. He kin be so skilful he kin sometimes get it withoot even askin. Jist his presence and actions alane kin make ye part wi yer tobacco, yer coffee, yer milk an anything else ye've goat that he husnae.

'Here pal, kin ye help us oot? Ye widnae huv a wee coffee fur us wid ye?'

'Naw.'

'Nae bother pal, kin ye geese a wee draw ae yer roll-up then? Embdae any sugar?'

The Coodgie never wants tae leave empty-haunded, nor kin he, the list will generally start aff wi tobacco an work its way doon tae sugar.

The Coodgie never replaces or pays back a debt, however, he will tell ye in the maist sincere fashion that he'll square ye up next week. The Coodgie kin think fast oan his feet. Whe ye chin him aboot a previous debt he'll make up some long-winded heart-wrenching speech in jist ower a second and it the same time huv a soorowful look aw ower his puss.

UNTITLED

A TIPPEXED VERSION OF A POEM FROM CHARLES REZNIKOFF'S HOLOCAUST

ANONYMOUS

Leaves
Among themselves
Were seven
Hiding leaves;
Two went up to the pit

With whips

They were ready to work
To rise and run,
Pushing their feet.
Still alive
And dead
Again

Everything on Merlene

James L

It could have been any other morning. She'd got up and left for work without me even noticing—except it wasn't. From the second I opened my eyes I had that battle inside between excitement and dread. Recently it had all been dread if anything but mostly I had been void of any feelings.

With no job to speak of, just the odd homer, very little money for anything and a wedding day approaching quicker than the speed of light. But that morning there seemed to be light at the end of this darkness. I'd a job to start come Monday, less than a week away.

At first I thought I would have needed to have turned it down. It was in Stirling and how the hell was I going to travel to Stirling every day? Then Auld Paul offered me £800, the exact money Young Paul wanted for his Orion. Her family were all bankers but even so this was a win-win situation.

It seemed simple: get a car, get a job, get money, get married then get on with life. Easy! Problem was in every easy plan there is one common denominator that mucks it all up—me. Now what was wrong with the Auld Yin handing over the cash to his son, her uncle, and me being handed the keys to the clapped out, overpriced vehicle to happiness. No, I'd to meet the git at the Clydesdale Bank at eleven a.m. and he'd give me the money. I'd then hold on to it until five p.m. and go round to Cousin Paul's when he comes home from work and give him it. Now there's a huge flaw in this plan—me with £800 up the toon and six hours to kill.

Anyone else would see the importance of not mucking this one up, too much at stake. That was the dread. The excitement was almost the same. Six hours with 800 quid and the bookies would be open. I could double or treble this with smart betting, give back the original £800, go to Ian Skelly's and buy a half decent car.

I didn't even wash. Out of bed, into yesterday's—or were they the day before's?—clothes and out of the house before nine a.m.

I loitered outside the bank for well over two hours (no hurry, eh Paul?) watching motors stop at the lights, thinking, 'Aye, a wee Golf', 'No, a wee Metro'. It passed the time but it seemed to have stood still waiting and waiting.

Then he appeared, all small talk and smiles. I squeezed a half smile but that was all he was getting. He had me over a barrel and was doing me no favours, lending me the cash to buy his son's squib and into the bargain I hated him, his son and any other human being with the same DNA flowing through them. I loved her a hundred and ten per cent but her family—vultures.

Her mother was the worst. An auld cow fae the schemes that had now met some half decent guy with a bit of pay and suddenly she had developed morals, you know, like an ex-smoker—'That's a disgusting habit.' She was now all, 'You wouldn't catch me drinking in the afternoon.' And, 'We've booked in for a fortnight in Butlin's.' She was so full of it she couldn't hear the whole scheme laughing.

Anyway. A quick lie, 'I need to pop down and see my dad.' And I was off.

Gone were any self-deluding thoughts that I wasn't going to the bookie's. The only question was what one. Not my regular. No doubt she'd be in looking for me during her lunch break and the last thing I wanted to do was let her down. I wanted to surprise her with my winnings! Positive mental attitude. I heard that Linford Christie say it on an advert and now it was my own personal mantra.

So here I am, 2.30 p.m., and already 5 x £20 bets down. Time to step up to £50s. First one kicks clear inside the final furlong. Home and hosed. This is going to be cool. 4.45, last race and I'm £400 down as the donkey I'd picked crashes through the first fence and decides to saunter roon. I'm screaming at the screen in the hope the jockey'll hear me and decide, 'I'll get going and win this for the wee man.' Hey hope springs eternal, whatever the f*** that means.

So it's off to the boozer. If I'm p***** then I won't feel such a 'huge disappointment' whilst I'm being told I am.

8.15, leaving the boozer and I clock the bookie's is still open. No night races. Why? So I venture over and they are covering the World Championship athletics. Hey, they bet on anything.

So I get the slip wrote out, count my cash and put £378 on Merlene Otty to win the 200m sprint. She'd lost the 100m, or so I was told by the resident pundit/jakey, and hello a photo finish with FloJo.

'She was in a photo for the 100m and Flo-Jo won,' says the auld joke-ball. Not really what I was wanting to hear. Then the result comes through—first Merlene Otty of Jamaica. Yee haa. £1134. The exact money paid out on my last ever bet. Got the car, got the job, got cash, got married...

... got caught with her pal, got divorced, but hey you can't win them all.

Untitled

Cathy R (HMP Styal)

Wandering like a lost soul
A white ghost
Upstairs and downstairs
In out of rooms
Putting chill into rooms
Making everyone shiver
They are spooked by it
They run away
Leaving me
What had I done wrong?
I saw an angel guardian's light
Shining in the distance
I tried to get there
But couldn't
I didn't need to worry
My guardian angel
Came to me
Like a big gold light
Twinkled in my eyes
Suddenly I felt
The glow in my cheeks
I felt tingling
I felt hot
The badness came out of me
The ghost had gone
There emerged
A bright positive woman
Who has confidence
Self-belief and happiness

Towards an End: A World Beyond

Free to Write's ambition has always been to allow inmates and ex-offenders to write about their lives and reflect on how they came to be here, and what series of actions might lift them to a better place. We wanted to produce a book that revealed that awareness to prison readers: stories told by you for you.

In this final selection of stories, our writers are plotting a new world in which the characters change trajectory, towards and into a free and natural world.

Shiela D suggests evolution is possible and Richard A draws a wonderful picture of humans in futile pursuits within a natural world that never changes, and this nobility of the natural world is clearly something that attracts many incarcerated writers, so, in 'Oyster Shells', Paul V makes us think more deeply about our position under the same 'early sun'.

Struggles

Shiela D (HMP Styal)

The boy removed the pupa from the tree
And felt the moth moving inside
He slowly broke the insect's casing free
The peered at the moth with pride
You're free now so I do not understand
Why have you not yet flown away?
Why are you still in the palm of my hand?
It's not the place for you to stay

The undeveloped wings could not extend
And the lad he became concerned
But he was unable to comprehend
That the moth's freedom must be earned
If left to struggle then the tiny veins
In its wings would have swelled with blood
If only he'd been allowed to remain
And work to break free as he should

The poor insect was a pathetic sight
Trying so hard to fly away
Instinct dictated that he must take flight
Or be fated to become prey
The moral of this story is quite clear
Though hardships in life may seem wrong
When all of our struggles can bring us to tears
In the end they can make us strong

August 14th (1977)

Richard A (HMP Frankland)

The shoreline is strewn with jagged and smooth rocks which are millions of years old, covered in periwinkles and fossils of molluscs; they seem to protrude like miniature mountains. Being grey, cracked and sedulous, slowly eroding with time by the salty water and being exposed to the elements, rocks shape shift into pebbles.

The waves endlessly glide to and fro and swish and swirl over and around the rocks swiftly, and the flowing rivers of water in-between the smaller rocks right up on the shoreline gradually make their way back into the swell of the sea, stretching far and wide over the horizon. Even the mackerel sky instils meditative absorption giving one the feeling of being connected to nature. That's all there is—the sky, the waves and the rocks plus that feeling of oneness with the sound of the sea—the expanse of the salty sea breeze.

The gulls bob on the water, soaring and flying above. You just know they belong here. The white waves and seagulls seem to blend together. They make this place connect with life and movement. Without them the waves and rocks might seem threatening to a person.

All the sea anglers have gone home and moved on. Patiently they use these shores to fish for cod, eel and sea bass in all types of weather, bringing with them flasks of tea and sandwiches. When the tide goes out it is a different place—with rocks and newly formed rock pools and sandy beaches. The rock pools are alive with crabs, hermit crabs, trapped fish and sometimes a lobster. The sea anemones pulsate and the tiny fish swim gracefully and deftly to avoid their predators. These pools are still compared to the sea where life beneath the surface is an art for survival.

The gold sand is covered in lugworm casts and seagulls looking for food such as shrimp or tiny crabs just below the surface. Sometimes there are mounds of sand where an angler has been digging for lugworm or ringworm for bait to catch his fish. In summer the beach is covered with umbrellas, deckchairs, people of all ages who laugh and scream with joy as they play at the water's edge with balls, splashing water at each other. Swimmers show off their prowess and kids play in the sand with a spade, filling buckets then turning them upside-down to produce sandcastles. Even the dogs are in glee searching up and down the sand. The ice cream man sets off his ringtone of music every now and then to let everyone know he's still trading. The sun seems good for the bathers. All of this bliss is a far cry from the days of the Titanic, the merchant ships being sunk by U-Boats, Normandy, the Longships, the nuclear submarines stealthily moving through the waters... Even Nelson had his glory at sea, but at a price. And why do most adults think of a shark when they are by the sea or at sea or in a boat, trawler, liner or yacht? Is it because they saw Jaws at the movies or on the telly? Yet it's good that the surfer shows no fear when he spearheads through a large curling wave.

When everyone has gone home there is just the sea, rocks, sky, sun and sandy beaches. In other seasons the place has another meaning and purpose, perhaps for the scuba diver, the geologist, the painter, the poet, an odd couple out walking their Labrador and underwater researchers—all vying for the space of privacy by or in the sea.

I once saw a photographer trying to capture a very fast moving jet in the azure sky, leaving a wake behind, at an angle where he got the sea in focus as well as the rocks and waves. The same photographer once told me he'd captured a full moon out in broad daylight on a sunny day with azure sky at this spot he was where we talked. I often wonder if there is a scientific name for that or is it one of those things which happen in nature.

To sit in a small house on the cliff top with my pipe in an old arm chair sinking into the earth and view this seascape I can't help but think of those galleons and watchers in those bird nests surveying the sea for land, the pirate ships and how it was then and how it is now, yet the tide stills goes in and out and people are still fascinated by the sea—its beaches, its rocks and the natural habitat of all the creatures above and below the surface. The sea has got it down to a fine art and has done for many centuries and no doubt will continue its magnificent quango long after we are all gone.

Oyster shells

Paul V (HMP Shrewsbury)

Early sun struggles through haar,
And milky cottages grip limpet-tight,
Like infants, to the sea-smashed cliffs.
Ancient, fortress-walled
Hives for workers of the sea.
Modest haddock hang beside the noble salmon,
Shining gold in equal death.
Outside all is quiet in the gentle breeze.
The jaundiced smoke that haunts
Terracotta chimneys, and steals down streets,
Gives only hints of delicious industry,
Whose product will go far and wide
To gourmet eateries in Paris or Rome,
And sawdust restaurants with oyster shells.

AUTHOR NOTES

GARETH CREER is the founder of Free to Write and was writer-in-residence at HMYOI Glen Parva and Merseyside Probation Services. He is the author of the novels *Skin and Bone*, *Cradle to Grave* and *Big Sky* (all published by Transworld), and has written five novels in the DI Staffe series for Faber and Faber under the pseudonym Adam Creed. He is also Head of Writing at Liverpool John Moores University.

ERWIN JAMES is a writer and columnist for *The Guardian*. He served twenty years of a life sentence in prison before his release in August, 2004. He is the author of *Life Inside: A Prisoner's Notebook* and *The Home Stretch: From Prison to Parole* (both published by Atlantic Books).

HANNAH PRIEST is an academic writer based in Manchester. She has published articles on popular literature and film, as well as medieval literature. She currently holds an Honorary Research Fellowship at the University of Manchester—where she gained her PhD in 2010—and works as a research assistant on the Free to Write project and anthology at Liverpool John Moores University. Under the name Hannah Kate, she is a poet and short story writer, and works as a freelance Creative Writing tutor, editor and book reviewer. Hannah is the founder of Hic Dragones, a small press based in North Manchester.

HELEN ROGERS lectures in English at Liverpool John Moores University. In 2013 her students will be developing a public blog called 'Criminal Lives', exploring real-life and fictional prison voices. This will be the companion site to http://www.writinglives.org, a research blog on working-class autobiography by English students at LJMU. Helen is currently writing a book called *Conviction: Prison Lives in the Nineteenth Century*. Her previous publications include *Women and the People: Authority, Authorship and the Radical Tradition in Nineteenth-Century England* (Ashgate) and *Gender and Fatherhood in the Nineteenth Century* (Palgrave), edited with Trev Broughton. She is also co-editor of the *Journal of Victorian Culture* (Routledge).

TAMSIN SPARGO is Reader in Cultural History and teaches Creative Writing at Liverpool John Moores University. Her books include *Wanted Man: The Forgotten Story of an American Outlaw* (Bloomsbury), *Reading the Past: Literature and History* (Palgrave), *Foucault and Queer Theory* (Icon) and *The Writing of John Bunyan* (Ashgate). She has written numerous articles and chapters on subjects ranging from post-secular theory to nonconformity and is currently writing a novel set in her native Cornwall.

ACKNOWLEDGEMENTS

THE EDITORS WOULD LIKE to thank the following organisations for their input, support and assistance with the Free to Write project and anthology: Writers in Prison Network, English PEN, Merseyside Probation Services, Liverpool City Libraries, Koestler Trust and Prisoners Education Trust. For support with historical research, the editors would like to thank the staff at the New York State Archive, New York Department of Corrections (including Auburn, Clinton and Matteawan facilities) and the Library of Congress. Thanks also to the writers-in-residence, teachers and librarians who assisted with securing consent and permissions for the publication of prisoners' work, particularly Harry Palmer, Michael Crowley, Kate Hendry, Cassandra Gilbert and Brenda Read-Brown. Thanks also to *STIR* magazine for assisting with examples of creative work from Scottish prisons.